Double
For
Your
Mourning

Gail Stevens

Double For Your Mourning
Copyright ©2008 by Gail Stevens
Printed in USA

Unless otherwise noted, all Scriptures are quoted from the New King James Version copyright 1982; Thomas Nelson, Inc.

Emphasis within the Scriptures are the authors.

Exalt Him Books
205 Skyline Road
Locust Grove, VA 22508
ExaltHim54@hotmail.com

Testimonies welcomed ☺
www.ExaltHimBooks.com

ISBN 978-0-9802422-0-1

Exalt Him Books

Dedication

This book is dedicated to my husband, Gary, who walks in concert with me in our Spiritual quest. And, to our children and their families for the richness they continually bring to our hearts. Most of all I write to those who have suffered loss: *"Look what the Lord can do!"*

Acknowledgements

Heartfelt appreciation to: Pastor Jack Hayford who first taught us to walk in God's ways; Pastor Patrick Bopp for currently shepherding our family, refueling my flame to write, and editing; Patty Howell who graciously provided her skill as a professional editor; Osvaldo Lara for his cover design; Ann Harrell's technical help; my daughter Anna for her graphic input; and to my family, friends and fellow saints at Raccoon Ford Christian Fellowship whose input helped shape the final rendition. May God continuously pour His rich blessings upon you.

God is not unjust to forget your work and labor of love which you have shown toward His name, in that you have ministered to the saints and do minister. *(Hebrews 6:10)*

Endorsement

$\mathcal{I}$ am more than happy to recommend Gail Stevens book, "Double For Your Mourning." Knowing Gail herself is a joy and it is always an uplift to ones spirit to be with her. Reading her book was a pleasure and an inspiration. The scriptural content is amazing. I believe her greatest gift in this book is sharing herself so vividly. She is open about her struggles and her victories both which can't help but be an encouragement to many. Sincerely,

Anna Hayford

Forewords

$\mathcal{T}$he story that unfolds in these pages is a labor of love. Any book is a labor of love, involving conception, gestation (pains and tears), and birth (presentation). More importantly, however, this book is a labor of God's love. It tells of His compassion, forgiveness and forbearance, patience, long-suffering and revelation. God's love, His heart and true nature were revealed when my wife, Gail, practiced the same attributes which God demonstrated through Christ Jesus. Jesus was the model, the example, which she chose to emulate during a difficult experience in our family.

The message is clear and unmistakable: If we follow God's example when faced with life's difficulties and burdens, He is faithful to redeem what might otherwise seem hopeless.

We trust that you, the reader, will be encouraged to seek and trust in God's redeeming love the next time you face a daunting situation or circumstance.

Gary Stevens, JD

$\mathcal{D}$ouble For Your Mourning is a modern-day parable. It is a story of redemption, faith, and hope in the midst of tragedy. It is a story of redemption, because the nature of God as Redeemer is clearly portrayed. It is a story of faith, because Kingdom principles are employed in ways that demonstrate thoughtful choices. It is a story of hope, because God is not a respecter of persons. What He has done for one, He will do for others!

Double For Your Mourning is an account of divine restoration. The use of kingdom principles guided Gail and Gary Stevens through their valley and into a saving knowledge of God.

The Stevens' journey is a pathway for many who will follow. The particular expression of God's redemption in their lives is extraordinary by any standard. It is one example of how God makes all things work together for good (*Romans 8:28*). The lesson is that God will redeem those who turn to Him in their time of need. While affirming the redemptive nature of the Father, it avoids any attempt to predict the nature of His kindness in other situations.

I was with Gail in Mexico when she first shared this story publicly. The pastor who translated was so overwhelmed by the faithfulness of God that he could not speak for extended periods of time. I am sure that this will be your experience as well. Gail and Gary are wonderful friends, people who are down to earth and funny, and believers who with good reason can say, "God will give *Double For Your Mourning*."

Patrick J. Bopp

Table of Contents

Introduction

As my husband, Gary, and I were being shaped by the events that changed the course of our lives, I had a sense that I was to document the wonderful ways the Lord was blessing us. The desire to encourage others suffering loss has been germinating inside me for many years.

I believe the release was delayed until I could articulate a clearer understanding of God's Word and His very nature. I had all but put aside my notion to write when, in the fall of 2006, Gary and I were asked to go with a team to minister to pastors in Saltillo, Mexico. As I prayed, the Lord began to confirm our going. The first thing to surface was a long forgotten dream to be part of a traveling ministry team. Next I recalled a vision I'd had of our church being at the hub of a wooden wagon wheel with the spokes representing ministry outreaches. I also sensed it was the beginning of a new season in our church with potential to produce good fruit in the Kingdom. The final confirmation came as I read, *"Go ye therefore, and teach all nations..." (Matthew 28:19 KJV).* While not sure how God would use us, we did know Jesus expects us to "teach" out of our living experiences. And, He not only engineers our goings, but promises to go with us. Gary prayed we would come home with "spiritual stretch marks." Most intimidating to me was the requirement that we share a personal testimony in one of the church services while in Mexico.

Adding to my uneasiness at the thought of speaking publicly was a desire to share something fresh. Then the Lord reminded me this story was "for such a time as this."

While sharing my testimony at Casa de Oracion, I was taken by surprise at the response of the very distinguished Pastor Pedro Gonzalez as my words clearly began to resonate in his heart. His emotions ranged from joyful laughter to tears of grief during the sad points. Sometimes it was 3-4 minutes before he could regain his composure to continue interpreting for me and I found myself consoling him. This greatly bolstered my confidence. Had he stood like a potted plant I would have wondered if my message was relevant. Over dinner he said, *"You must write this testimony in a book,"* and I knew in my heart it was true. However, it was our own pastor, Patrick Bopp, who gave the final impetus by asking me to share this testimonial in our church on Mother's Day and to *"have 'the book' ready."* Gary was a great encouragement and helped see me through this process.

On February 2, 1979 our odyssey began. Gary and I had been married close to twenty years. We had three sons, Lance, Todd, and Shawn, who were eighteen, sixteen, and two years old, respectively. This is a story of God's redemption in our family. God will redeem your situation in keeping with the desires of your heart. There is no limit to His creative redemptive ability.

To God be the glory for great things He has done. I pray the words of my testimony will encourage you to realize that when we invite God in, He becomes intimately involved in the details of our lives. Come with me to see God's blessing and redemption of a most difficult and heart wrenching time. The decision I made in that moment changed the course of my family's life forever and continues to take my husband and me on an adventure far beyond our dreams.

...I will turn their mourning to joy, will comfort them, and make them rejoice rather than sorrow.   (Jeremiah 31:13)

Chapter One

"Tell My Dad I'm Okay"

The night was still, the streets wet from a gentle rain, and a chill was in the air from the snow-covered foothills behind our home. I was still propped up in my warm, cozy bed when I dozed off to sleep. I had been working to finish one last door prize, a latch hook pillow featuring a soccer player. Some 300 guests would be in attendance the following evening at a dinner/dance fundraiser I had organized for my soccer team. My husband, Gary, left home at 11:15 p.m. to pick up our sixteen-year old son, Todd, who was attending a sweet-sixteen party given for one of his classmates at Los Angeles Baptist High School. The phone rang and awoke me. I was surprised to see it was 1:00 a.m. *"An accident? Is he* (my husband) *alert and thinking clearly?"* "Yes," was the nurse's response. No mention was made of Todd. *"Please ask him if he picked up our son Todd."* When she didn't call back I sent our eldest son, Lance, to get his brother. After calling and questioning the nurse again, I was finally told, *"Your son was taken to another hospital."* I called Northridge Hospital to get a report on Todd. I gave my name and asked to speak with the doctor. In the background I heard an anxious sounding whisper, *"It's Mrs. Stevens."* And, instead of a doctor, a policeman came on the phone. Being an operating room nurse myself, I sensed I was getting the run around. The policeman was very polite, but firm, in telling me I was most needed at West Park Hospital with my husband and he would meet me there as soon as possible. He would not give me a report on my son. At this point I became very agitated, and insisted that he tell me Todd's condition on the phone. He claimed this was against policy. I took a deep breath and asked point blank, *"Is he dead?"*

I shall never forget the sinking feeling in my stomach followed by waves of nausea. In the following months I relived that feeling dozens of times as I recounted that call. A surge of emotion would begin in the pit of my stomach and flow up through my heart to my head and fill me with grief.

After receiving the news of Todd, I slowly picked up the phone to call my parents and a sense of total helplessness overtook me. Over and over I repeated to my mom and dad, *"I don't know what I am going to do. What am I going to do?"* God said, *"I want you to trust me in your times of trouble, so I can rescue you, and you can give Me glory"* (*Psalm 50:15 The Living Bible -TLB*). I began to work out this principle the very night I arrived in the emergency room at West Park Hospital. I soon found Gary didn't know of the death of our son, Todd, and that I would be the one who had to tell him. My thoughts raced, *"How can I do this? No, I can't do this alone, I need God's help."* This realization changed the direction of our lives forever.

Gary had picked up Todd, and they were en route home from the party. A car, driven by a nineteen-year-old man who'd had too many beers and was driving way too fast, crossed the center median and became airborne. His car hit the driver's side of our vehicle. Gary and Todd were in the far right lane of a four-lane road. My husband was pinned in the car. When he became conscious he struggled, trying to reach Todd. He repeatedly called out to him, unaware he had died on impact. It was a miracle Gary survived. Only five inches of space remained between the driver's seat and the steering wheel. The wheel severely lacerated Gary's face, caused a head injury and compressed his chest. His right knee was also badly injured. The car was so mangled that the Jaws of Life had to be used to get him out.

As family and friends gathered in the waiting room in the wee hours of the night, I knew I had to reach someone who knew God. I tried to call the friend who first invited us to church, but she wasn't home. Then I called a Sunday school teacher of a church we had attended for four or five years. However, at this time, we hadn't been in church regularly for two years. Church had been, in some respects, a social club for us. We knew nothing of a personal relationship with Jesus and very little about the Bible. Thankfully that Sunday school teacher came to the hospital and went with me as I told Gary of Todd's death. Gary's first words to me were, *"I'm sorry, I'm sorry, Gail."*

Gary seemed to blame himself, because he was driving. I felt guilty as I had insisted Todd come home at the appointed time when he called asking to stay a little later. Lance thought he was to blame, because he encouraged Todd to change his plans and go to the party. It is best not to let the "if only" author (we know who he is) torment you.

Great friends of ours from Gary's law school days, Joe and Lorraine, drove our youngest son, Shawn, then two years and nine months old, and me to West Park Hospital. Joe and Lorraine then escorted me as Gary was taken by ambulance to Valley Presbyterian Hospital. I worked there in the operating room at the time and wanted familiar surgeons caring for him. Gary underwent eight hours of surgery on his right knee and face as I wandered in and out of the surgical suite and recovery room.

At some point, Lorraine asked if there was someplace she could lie down. The nurse let her lie on a small, narrow gurney. During that time she saw a vision of Todd standing beside the gurney and he said to her *"Tell my Dad I'm okay and I know it wasn't his fault."* As Lorraine relayed the vision to my sister Danya, a Christian, she got goose bumps and tears came to her eyes. Later, relating the story to me, Lorraine said she laid down because she was cold and uncomfortable, not sleepy. She still remembered the picture very vividly. The Lord works in mysterious ways and I sensed this was a touch from Him to comfort Gary and me.

Chapter Two
Turn Your Face to God

Deep in my heart is a desire to give hope to those who have lost a child. Let me tell you how the Lord restored "double for our mourning" after the loss of our sixteen-year-old son, Todd Michael Stevens.

Instead of your shame (loss) you shall have double honor, and instead of confusion they shall rejoice in their portion. Therefore in their land they shall possess double; Everlasting joy shall be theirs.   *(Isaiah 61:7)*

Other than life itself, a child has to be the most precious gift one receives from God. The bonding in love begins the moment you become aware of conception and blossoms as you look with wonderment at the baby you cuddle in your arms. It is an extremely humbling experience to see God's creative miracle entrusted to your care. Love flows and continually deepens through the various stages of childhood. How proud you are of them. Children become an extension of your whole life, your whole being. Your thoughts and efforts are focused on them day and night.

Words are inadequate to describe the anguish I felt in losing Todd to a premature death. Terrible wrenching, pulling and tearing made me feel as though a large part of my heart had been ripped out. But I can tell you first hand:

"...the Lord your God is gracious and merciful, and will not turn His face from you if you return to Him"

(2 Chronicles 30:9).

David said in *Psalm 121:1-5* *"I will lift up my eyes to the hills—From whence comes my help? My help comes from the Lord, who made heaven and earth. He will not allow your foot to be moved; He who keeps you will not slumber. Behold, He who keeps Israel shall neither slumber nor sleep. The Lord is your keeper..."*

My husband and I chose to turn our faces and look to God. We did not focus on the person or cause of our crisis. I had no desire to go to his trial and today I don't even recall the young man's name. Somehow I held no unforgiveness toward him, which even to this day I find amazing since I didn't have a personal relationship with Jesus at the time of the accident. I do remember feeling compassion toward him. I knew in my heart he had a great deal to process and deal with. He was responsible for Todd's death and Gary's injuries. In addition, two girls had been in his car with him. One, who was seventeen-years old, was thrown out of the car and died three weeks later from massive head injuries. Neither she nor Todd were wearing seatbelts.

The driver received a cut on his face. His Catholic priest visited me and was somewhat amazed by my attitude. He asked if I would be willing to visit the young man. I said I would consider it. Instead of taking responsibility for his actions, he told his priest that the car's steering had malfunctioned. Interestingly, a few months earlier he had totaled another car in a single car accident.

Forgiveness allowed us not to harbor any bitterness. The Word tells us to:

"Pursue peace with all men, and holiness, without which no one will see the Lord: looking diligently lest anyone fall short of the **grace** *of God; lest any root of bitterness springing up cause trouble, and by this many become defiled..." (Hebrews 12:14-15).*

Grace is His unmerited favor and spiritual blessing and, as you will discover, our family experienced His grace.

Another passage states, *"And the Lord restored Job's losses when he prayed for his friends. Indeed the Lord gave Job twice as much as he had before" (Job 42:10).* Job's friends had not treated him kindly. Although we don't sanction the poor behavior of people, when we forgive then pray for them it allows God to start working in the situation. He is the God of redemption. *Proverbs 20:22 TLB* commands, *"Don't repay evil for evil. Wait for the Lord to handle the matter."* I Peter 3:9 tells us not to return *"...evil for evil...but...blessing,*

11

knowing that you were called to this, that you may inherit a blessing."

I like to think of unforgiveness as a weed in my garden. The longer I ignore it the deeper its roots grow and the more difficult it is to pull out. If left long enough it begins to take over, crowding my garden, robbing it of nutrients and making it look poorly. In my body, unforgiveness can lead to illness, block healing, rob peace and alter my way of relating to others. It may also keep me from some of the promises of God, limit His work through me, and be a hindrance to my prayers. To be in right standing we must forgive.

For the eyes of the Lord are on the righteous, and His ears are open to their prayers; but the face of the Lord is against those who do evil.   *(I Peter 3:12)*

Forgiveness is a choice I must make out of pure obedience to the Lord's Word. Even though the appropriate feelings may not be in my heart, I choose to forgive as an act of my will. Then and most importantly, I must sincerely pray according to the Word in *Matthew 5:44, "...love your enemies, bless those who curse you, do good to those who hate you, and pray for those who spitefully use you and persecute you."*

When I earnestly pray asking God to bless the offending person or situation, I notice a soothing peaceful feeling begins to come into my heart to ease the pain or help me see things in a new light. Anger and hurt are released and my mind does not continually return to the events. Sometimes I must go a step further and find a suitable scripture to recite each time I start ruminating. When peace comes then I know I have successfully placed the problem in God's hands. We must step out of the way so the Lord can work in the situation. This scripture helps me:

"... *'Vengeance is Mine, I will repay,' says the Lord* "
(*Romans 12:19*).

The Lord always forgives us and He gives us ample warning of the consequence of not forgiving others. Jesus relates in a parable: "*...I forgave you all that debt...Should you not also have had compassion on your fellow servant, just as I had pity on you? And his master was angry, and delivered him to the torturers until he should pay all that was due to him. So My heavenly Father also will do to you if each of you, from his heart, does not forgive his brother his trespasses*" (*Matthew 18:32-35*). Ouch!

I love the word picture Corrie ten Boom provides. She found herself having sleepless nights for weeks even after she tried forgiving someone of what they had done to her. However, she was still moved by emotions when she thought about it. She shared her struggles with her pastor. He told her to look up at the bell tower in the church. He pointed out the bell would continue to ring even after the person ringing it let go of the rope. In time, though, the bell would slowly wind down until it was silent. Let go of the rope as you forgive.

"...with God all things are possible"

(Matthew 19:26).

Gary and I chose to turn our face to God which allowed us to possess an inner peace and joy unlike any we had ever known before.

Chapter Three
True Nature of God

he Spirit of the Lord is upon Me, because the Lord has anointed Me to bring good news to the suffering and afflicted. He has sent Me to comfort the broken-hearted, to announce liberty to captives and to open the eyes of the blind. He has sent Me to tell those who mourn that the time of God's favor to them has come, and the day of His wrath to their enemies. To all who mourn in Israel* He will give: Beauty for ashes; Joy instead of mourning; Praise instead of heaviness. (Isaiah 61:1-3 TLB)

It is imperative to have an accurate picture of God's true nature in the midst of a trial. One must understand it is not God who is against us in life. To glibly assert *"God is in control"* as though it might be soothing to a person in a crisis, ultimately places blame on God. This view reflects a limited understanding of the scriptures and is an affront to God's absolute goodness. God made a sovereign choice to give man dominion on earth.

Then God blessed them, and God said to them, 'Be fruitful and multiply; fill the earth and subdue it; have dominion

---

* Israel (or Zion) is used figuratively to denote God's Kingdom. *Psalm 125:1; Hebrews 12:22; Revelation 14:1.*

over the fish of the sea, over the birds of the air, and over every living thing that moves on the earth.' (Genesis 1:28)

The heaven, even the heavens, are the Lord's; But the earth He has given to the children of men.   (Psalm 115:16)

Success is dependent upon our own self-government in obedience to God's laws. Most of our difficulties are the result of man's sin and direct attacks by our adversary, Satan.

Please know God is not the author of our trials, nor does He send or allow accidents and diseases to befall us. He loves us unconditionally. Even our sin does not affect His heart toward us. (This is not to say sin is without consequences.) He is our Daddy and great is His faithfulness in that role.

Long ago, even before He made the world, God chose us to be His very own, through what Christ would do for us; He decided then to make us holy in His eyes, without a single fault—we who stand before Him covered with His love. His unchanging plan has always been to adopt us into His own family by sending Jesus Christ to die for us. And He did this because He wanted to! Now all praise to God for His wonderful kindness to us and His favor that He has poured out upon us, because we belong to His dearly loved Son. So overflowing is His kindness towards us that He took away all our sins through the blood of His Son, by

16

whom we are saved; and He has showered down upon us the richness of His grace—for how well He understands us and knows what is best for us at all times.

(Ephesians 1:4-8 TLB)

Jesus said, *"The thief does not come except to steal, and to kill, and to destroy. I have come that they may have life, and that they may have it more abundantly. I am the good shepherd. The good shepherd gives His life for the sheep"*

(John 10:10-11).

It tells us in *I John 4:8 "...God is love."* Would you afflict a loved one to get their attention or teach them a lesson? Neither does God. Jesus teaches us to pray, *"Your kingdom come. Your will be done on earth as it is in heaven"* (Matthew 6:10). His will does not include sickness and accidents as there are none in heaven. *"Every good gift and every perfect gift is from above, and comes down from the Father of lights, with whom there is no variation or shadow of turning."*

(James 1:17)

As I shall chronicle later in this book, following Todd's death we spent over eight years at The Church on the Way, in Van Nuys, California. It was a time of great spiritual learning and growth. Recently, after having encountered a great deal of confusion about God's nature even amongst Christians, we reached out to our much loved former pastor,

Jack Hayford.* Although it had been fourteen years since we had attended his church, Pastor Jack very graciously clarified our thinking. Here are excerpts from his letter to us that we found exceptionally helpful.

You're thinking right when you reject those extremes inherent in an interpretation of God's sovereignty as accepting sin, death and evil's impacting of human experience by saying (basically) 'God be glorified, He's in charge—even of the destructive things that happen to people!' This order of camouflaged fatalism proposes to be exalting God's greatness by this posture. The fact is, of course, God is great, all-wise, all-knowing and all-powerful. But their approach breaks down in the fact of the exaggerated notions they propose to interpret God's sovereignty as including. And while we reject their approach, never let anyone suggest we believe God isn't 'in charge,' (and certainly not interpret us as reducing an appropriate emphasis on His sovereign will and power). The problem centers in their completely overlooking or negating the role of human choice.

This posture is a necessity of this non-biblical system that avows all human choice is a predestined result of God's earlier foreordained choices. Nonetheless, we DO hold that God has not resigned control of the ultimate

---

* Jack W. Hayford, D.Litt, Founder and Chancellor of The King's College and Seminary, Los Angeles, CA / Pastor, The Church on the Way, Van Nuys, CA

destiny of earth and humankind, but that He is taking it back via redemption's processes, and via the responses of those humans who chose to open to His Son, His salvation and His Kingdom. The bottom line is rooted in our conviction that insofar as earth and humankind are concerned, God's sovereign will has been manifest in His choice to delegate the responsibility for earth's affairs and human activities to mankind. All that distills in our world is, then, not the choice of God but the result of the choices of fallen man—and the added evil actions of satan under whose temporary sway this present world is manipulated.

In the meantime, God is at work—through Christ, via the Church and by the power of the Holy Spirit— sovereignly exhibiting His mighty grace and power wherever it is invited by the choices of the redeemed.

In Him, Jack W. Hayford

One area of difficulty may be our ability to relate to God as a loving Father. Our view of Him may have been skewed by our upbringing. The natural tendency is to compare the Creator Father God with the traits of our earthly father and this was God's original intent. Unfortunately, through the generations as sin entered their hearts, man wandered farther away from God. A father may have been physically or emotionally absent in one's life causing us to miss a father's love, affirmation, and protection. God desires to fill that empty void deep inside each of us that cries out for

Daddy's love. Our heavenly Father will never stop loving us. You were created for His glory.

> *Moreover, because of what Christ has done we have become gifts to God that He delights in, for as part of God's sovereign plan we were chosen from the beginning to be His...God's purpose in this was that we should praise God and give glory to Him for doing these mighty things for us...* (Ephesians 1:11-12 TLB)

David said, "*I will praise You, for I am fearfully and wonderfully made; Marvelous are Your works, and that my soul knows very well...Your eyes saw my substance, being yet unformed. And in Your book they were all written. The days fashioned for me, when as yet there were none of them. How precious also are Your thoughts to me, O God! How great is the sum of them! If I should count them, they would be more in number than the sand...*" (Psalm 139:14, 16-18).

Jeremiah 29:11 states: "*For I know the thoughts that I think toward you, says the Lord, thoughts of peace and not of evil, to give you a future and a hope.*"

Father God longs to have fellowship with us just as we long for fellowship with our own family and children. But He, having created us with a free will, waits patiently for us to pursue Him. His arms are open waiting to embrace and pour out the abundance of His love on us. It is hard to fathom the depth of love He has for us.*

But as it is written: 'Eye has not seen, nor ear heard, nor have entered into the heart of man the things which God has prepared for those who love Him.' (I Corinthians 2:9)

Another area that raises a question is the issue of health. *"Beloved, I pray that you may prosper in all things and be in health just as your soul prospers."(3 John 2)* Other scriptures speak of abundant life, living well and long on the earth, and of glorifying God in our bodies. Why then do some precious saints of God get heart disease, cancer, diabetes or other wasting diseases? And why, in spite of prayer, don't some get the healing Jesus provided for us at the cross? There are many answers to this conundrum and mysteries we may never understand until we get to heaven. However, in my passion for nutrition research and out of a need that arose over four years ago in our own lives, a wealth of interesting, even startling information has been uncovered. I have found that some diseases common in the United States are largely non-existent in other countries due to their dietary practices.

It is interesting to note that in the early 1900s cancer was so rare that it was conceivable that a doctor might never run across a case in the entire duration of his practice. Heart disease was not even mentioned in most medical textbooks

*See *Prayers* for blessing children page 141

prior to 1900. Today cancer and heart disease are the leading causes of death in the United States. And, starting with the very young, obesity and diabetes have become a major concern. The universal truth that "we reap what we sow" very much applies to our physical bodies. Good nutrition equals good health. God receives glory when we are well. *"For you were bought at a price; therefore glorify God in your body and in your spirit, which are God's."*

(I Corinthians 6:20)

God laid out His plan for man's food in *Genesis 1:29.* Could it be most of us have moved far away from the original way God intended for us to eat and don't even know it?

My people are destroyed for lack of knowledge. Because you have rejected knowledge, I also will reject you from being priest for Me...   *(Hosea 4:6)*

God wants us to learn and exercise good stewardship over our bodies, His temple of the Holy Spirit. The wonderful news is, He has provided readily available foods not only to prevent disease but to help us get well if we should find ourselves with a menacing diagnosis.*

---

* Please see *Nutrition Notes* on page 123

Chapter Four
Searching For Him

The most important thing our former Sunday school teacher did was to put us in touch with the church he was then attending—The Church on the Way (TCOTW) in Van Nuys, California. The first church service I attended was the Wednesday after the accident. A Spirit-filled Episcopal priest, Dennis Bennett, was speaking about his best friend who had just lost his seventeen-year-old son in a boating accident. He taught how faithful God was to turn what was meant for evil into good. And, that God does not want or cause terrible losses to come to us. Although there were a lot of facets Gary and I did not understand, we did not try to figure out all the answers immediately. We just started to learn about God through His Word and fellowship.

Then you will call upon Me and go and pray to Me, and I will listen to you. And you will seek Me and find Me, when you search for Me with all your heart. (Jeremiah 29:12-13)

...The Lord is with you while you are with Him. If you seek Him, He will be found by you; but if you forsake Him, He will forsake you. (2 Chronicles 15:2)

Psalm 91:1-11 is a wonderful promise to us:

"He who **dwells** in the secret place of the Most High shall abide under the shadow of the Almighty.

I will say of the Lord, 'He is my refuge and my fortress; My God, in Him I will trust.'

Surely He shall deliver you from the snare of the fowler and from the perilous pestilence.

He shall cover you with His feathers, and under His wings you shall take refuge; His truth shall be your shield and buckler.

You shall not be afraid of the terror by night, nor of the arrow that flies by day, nor of the pestilence that walks in darkness, nor of the destruction that lays waste at noon day.

A thousand may fall at your side, and ten thousand at your right hand; but it shall not come near you.

Only with your eyes shall you look, and see the reward of the wicked.

Because you have made the Lord, who is my refuge, even the Most High, your dwelling place, no evil shall befall you, nor shall any plague come near your dwelling; for He shall give His angels charge over you to keep you in all your ways."

We must make a decision to **"dwell"** and thus live under His protective covering.

Although we had never attended TCOTW, they embraced us, made all the arrangements for a memorial service for Todd at the church, and officiated at the funeral service and interment at Oak Park Chapel Cemetery the next day. This was the first funeral I had ever attended. With Gary hospitalized many decisions fell to me. This included switching funeral homes (the first one tried to take advantage of me by only offering an extremely expensive casket or a plain unpainted pine box) and finding a burial site. My dad helped guide me. The doctors agreed to release Gary early and services were delayed a week so Gary could attend. We took him directly from the hospital to the church in a wheelchair. When we entered the sanctuary Todd's dearly loved piano teacher was playing his favorite piece, "The Entertainer." And in some ways this song title described Todd's personality. Roger Thrower (a Christian songwriter and pastor) composed a special song, which he sang and played on his guitar. At least fourteen people acknowledged receiving Jesus as the invitation was given. Praise the Lord! As the service ended, Pastor Lee Jones instructed each of the approximately 300 people to come forward and simply give Gary and me a heartfelt hug.

Pulling up to Oak Park Chapel for the funeral the next day, provided me with a picture indelibly printed on my heart. The lawns outside the charming stone chapel were covered with people as there was not enough room inside. Todd's soccer coach and friends spoke, another played his guitar, one read a poem he had written for Todd, and we all filed by Todd's casket for a final goodbye. We praise God for TCOTW because they nurtured, loved and taught us God's Word.

Gary and I attended church every time the doors opened, and like sponges, soaked up everything we could. We listened to the 8:00 a.m. early morning Sunday service on the radio while driving to church. We went to services Sunday morning and on Sunday and Wednesday evenings. Gary went monthly to men's growth seminars. And there were extra teachings as Servants Council members. All were taught by Pastor Jack Hayford. We also participated in special Sunday school series taught by varying pastoral staff.

Church filled a huge gap in our lives. I fondly remember how our hearts were flooded with joy that first holiday season at TCOTW. It seemed like one big celebration from Thanksgiving to New Year's Eve. I loved the festive decorations. We even had a giant gingerbread house in the foyer one year. Our family enjoyed all of the many special services. Each year brought varied and exciting ways of celebrating our Lord Jesus. At "Family Night around the Christmas tree" we actually strung red and green colored popcorn in church, Pastor Jack played his marimba, the church band played traditional Christmas carols and the children's choirs sang. There also were special musicals with professional accompaniment. I recall the time carolers in 1900s costumes sang around lampposts in the aisles. Several repeat performances were required to accommodate all who wanted to attend. There was never a charge (a blessing to us at the time) for special events and you could count on an altar call at every gathering. Both encouraged us to bring unsaved friends. My husband and I were baptized in water and with the Holy Spirit* within a few months. We are eternally grateful for our foundation in Christ established by the teachings of Pastor Jack Hayford who shall always remain in our hearts as a dear friend.

---

* See *Holy Spirit* page 115

Chapter Five
Heavenly Ubiquitous
Gifts of Sensitivity

During our initial grieving the most effective form of comfort was a simple, heartfelt hug. Two years after our loss, I was still so moved by this newfound greeting that I wrote a letter to our pastor and the staff at TCOTW. Below is most of the text and I include it because hugs were extremely relevant to our healing.

Dear Pastor Jack and Staff at The Church on the Way,

I want you to know how the love of God personally reached my husband and me through the ministry of The Church on the Way. Although not members of the church at the time, we were taken in like little lambs and have been nurtured and growing. My husband and I are the happiest we have ever been in our married life. All around us, family, friends and business reflect this.

This love story began with a hug—an expression to us of God's love and strength. A hug felt as though He Himself was embracing us and we knew it instantly. There was an immediate transference of the weight of our burden being lifted and shared by the giver. Pent up emotions that made me feel like I was walking on thin ice that was about to shatter at any moment would be replaced with a deep peace in my heart by a timely ministered hug. The hug seemed to represent an extension of God's arms touching and supporting us. Throughout our initial adjustment period a hug was the single most comforting support given us. The hugs said 'I love you, God loves you, I will share your burden with you, I will help you, you can lean on me, I Am is with you.'

Our home was wall to wall flowers and plants. For three full weeks the telephone rang day and evening it seemed with out a break. We did not have to prepare a meal for two months. For three months a day didn't go by with out a card or letter. Approximately 300 people came to the memorial service at TCOTW. Over 300 were at the funeral at Oak Park Memorial Chapel the following day. We were deeply moved by this overwhelming outpouring of affection over the loss of our 16 year old son, Todd. Through it all, again I want to say, the single thing that comforted us most was a well administered hug. The first thing I want to do when we meet again is embrace that boy, something seldom done in recent years. It is one regret I have. We loved him deeply, he knew that, but why couldn't we express it freely? Sounds simple, but how often do we really hug those closest to us?

Hugging was kind of new to us at the time and I wonder why this should have been. Hugs must be a very old tradition and a very basic human need. What happened through the centuries that made us hesitant to use this valuable tool? A hug by itself is much more expressive than a kiss even in marriage. In fact a kiss practically loses meaning when not administered with a hug. I can't think of any age or situation

30

when a hug can't be effective and necessary for building health and happiness. A hug can melt an ornery child in a matter of seconds when all else seems to fail. It says I sure do love you to a parent, grandparent or elderly friend when we find words hard to express. A hug puts a twinkle in the eyes like nothing else I know.

This great rediscovery of ours was initiated by Pastor Lee Jones, the best expert we found. His timely hugs lifted our heavy hearts many times without a word spoken. It all started at the memorial service when he instructed each person there to come forward and one by one embrace us. I call hugs: "Heavenly Ubiquitous Gifts of Sensitivity."

Gail Stevens

Chapter Six
All Things Work Together

While we were definitely being blessed in so many ways, my heart still ached because I did not know if Todd was with Jesus. Lance, our eldest, had been baptized when we had attended the first church. He took this initiative independent of us. Neither Todd, nor Gary, nor I had followed suit.

One night, a month after the funeral, we were watching Todd's favorite movie, "The Sound of Music." My thoughts turned to him. I dashed up to his room to look for a report he had been feverishly preparing on the Sioux Indians. I opened his desk drawers and was amazed to find Todd's testimony. It was written about three months prior to his death for Mrs. Crowell's Bible II class at Los Angeles Baptist High School. He based it on *Romans 8:30 TLB:*

"And having chosen us, He called us to come to Him; and when we came, He declared us 'not guilty,' filled us with Christ's goodness, gave us right standing with himself, and promised us His glory."

"Romans Essay"

*This essay is very hard to do because Romans is full of so much knowledge that has helped me and can be applied to my life. The teaching that left the greatest impression on me is **8:30**, the teaching that I am not guilty before God because of Jesus. Even though I have made many mistakes and sins in the past, I am not condemned. No one can condemn me from God's grace.*

I feel that this is wonderful and I should let my friends in on the love Christ has for us. Christ must love me so much, anyone that would die so that I may have life must love me! Just thinking about that gives me feelings of his love flowing through me.

Being cleansed makes me feel good. My sins have been scratched from the record. Knowing this puts a new spark into my life and the way I act and also the way I treat others.

Todd Stevens *

Running for my Bible, I looked up the verse and immediately realized it was part of the same scripture Pastor Lee Jones had read at Todd's memorial service. He had never met Todd. I clearly remembered these words being spoken from *Romans 8:28, 31 "And we know that all things work together for good to those who love God......If God is for*

---

* Todd's hand-written testimony is on page 36. (Ivy and picture added by me for Christmas card insert).

us, who can be against us?" I was flooded with joy, jumping up and down and as you can imagine, walked around on a cloud for days. Todd's Bible teacher gave him a "B" on his paper but I know God gave him an "A." I sent a copy back to her and she told me she was certainly going to get to know her students much better.

Stevens Todd
Bible II per 5
Mrs. Crowell

Romans Essay

This essay is very hard to do because Romans is full of so much knowledge that has helped me and can be applied to my life. The teaching that left the greatest impression on me is 8:36 the teaching that I am not guilty before God because of Jesus. Even though I have made many mistakes and sins in the past, I am not condemned. No one can condemn me from Gods grace.

I feel that this is wonderful and I should let my friends in on the love Christ has for us. Christ must love me so much, anyone that would die so that I may have life must love me! Just thinking about that gives me feelings of his love flowing through me.

Being cleansed makes me feel good. My sins have been scratched from the record. Knowing this puts a new spark into my life and way I act and also the way I treat others.

A few months later in the sanctuary at church, I saw a vision of Todd kneeling at the feet of Jesus. I can still picture it. There is no better feeling than knowing your child is with the Lord. While not having this comfort would be difficult, it should never keep anyone from seeking the Lord. He waits to pour out His love and blessings on you. Some decisions for Christ (such as Todd's) are made without our knowledge or perhaps at the last minute. Todd's interest in spiritual things was not apparent at the time of his death. He was a typical sixteen-year-old and we would not have known he accepted Jesus were it not for finding his testimony paper. The only visible signs of change we noticed were improved study habits and grades and his resolve to become an orthodontist.

The one professional picture of our three sons was taken just a few weeks before Todd's death. The appointment was almost missed because Shawn fell in the bathtub cutting his lower lip and required stitches to repair it. This happened two days before the photo shoot. His lip was so discolored and swollen I decided to cancel. However the photo studio was very popular and not very flexible. The booking lady sternly warned, if I didn't come for this sitting, we could not have another appointment for at least six months. I took the three boys. I never notice the lip when looking at this sentimental photograph today.

Lance, Shawn and Todd (right)

Chapter Seven
Healing and Salvation

When Jesus went to the cross He provided a way for our salvation, which included eternal life, an abundance of blessings here on earth, and healing for our physical bodies. We must believe and receive them as gifts freely provided by Him. His work on earth was completed at the cross.

At one time, Gary and I believed we were Christians; but, sitting in church did not make us one. Each of us had to pray and personally invite Jesus into his life. One must believe in his heart that Jesus is the Son of God, and repent of his sins.

One of the most touching ways the Lord brought us closer to Himself was manifested through a phone call from people we hardly knew. We met Neil and Connie two and a half years prior to the loss of Todd at a Christian Legal Society conference in Colorado Springs. When asked if anyone had an anniversary that day the four of us stood up finding we had married the same day in the same year. And we did a little sightseeing together. I'd had no other contact with them in the interim. Gary made one brief visit to the Markva home in Virginia while participating in a Presidential Prayer Breakfast in Washington, D.C. As this couple prayed with him, he felt a touch of the Holy Spirit for the first time.

Upon hearing of the accident they telephoned and talked with us for an hour. I found it hard to believe people who barely knew us would reach out to us in that manner. At that time, long-distance phone calls were very expensive.

Neil and Connie Markva not only called to console us, but also invited us to visit them in their home in Virginia. Not knowing them well, I didn't want to leave the comfort of my home to go to an unfamiliar environment. Gary on the other hand was excited by the invitation, and other friends strongly encouraged us. I felt coerced into the trip. When the extreme swelling went down in Gary's leg a cast was put on. The week after the cast was taken off, we flew to Virginia.

The first evening Neil said, *"I just want to make sure all the bases are covered."* He had us turn to *Romans 10:9-10*:

"...if you confess with your mouth the Lord Jesus and believe in your heart that God has raised Him from the dead, you will be saved. For with the heart one believes unto righteousness, and with the mouth confession is made unto salvation."

We prayed and I believe it was the first time someone led me in a salvation prayer* to personally ask Jesus into my heart. Gary had prayed at age thirteen in vacation bible school. As Connie and Neil sowed into our lives day and

---

*Salvation page 109

night, I began to get really excited. Finally, the things of God started making sense to me. It was as if lights were turning on here and there over every situation. I began to recognize how the Lord had been intimately involved in our lives since the moment we first looked to Him. The Word of God came alive and we had a hunger and thirst to soak it up. We listened to the Bible on tapes in the car and while falling asleep each night. Prior to our loss of Todd, I thought of the Bible as archaic, difficult to read and even more difficult to understand. Suddenly, I became fascinated with all the wisdom and practicality of the Word of God. I wanted to give a Bible to everybody and to this day I still love to buy and give Bibles.

While we visited with the Markvas, God touched our grieving hearts and healed Gary's body in a supernatural way. During a home church meeting, I sat in the back of the room kind of enjoying myself when suddenly waves of grief overwhelmed me. No one in the room was aware of this, except God, of course. A young man coming in late and knowing nothing of our situation, stood and said, *"I sense the presence of mourning here."* To say I was shocked, is putting it mildly. *"How did he know?"* Two chairs were placed in the center of the room, and we sat there as people laid hands on us to pray for our broken hearts. The next Sunday we attended a communal gathering of several home churches and the same young man spoke again, seemingly out of the blue, and said, *"God is healing someone's right* knee." God spoke to us through that young man to show that He cared and knew our needs. I now know this is called a "word of knowledge." He did not have prior knowledge of Gary's knee injury which Dr. Miller, the orthopedic surgeon, claimed was the worst he'd ever seen. The tendons and muscles had to be reattached with wires and half of his knee cap had to be removed. Well, praises be to God, we walked all over Washington, D.C. and Gary had no problem with his leg.

Through Pastor Jack Hayford's teaching, we clearly came to understand and believe every "Word" in the Bible was inspired by God and is just as useful for us today as when it was written. The Word of God is timeless.

Jesus Christ is the same yesterday, today, and forever.
(Hebrews 13:8)

The grass withers, the flower fades, But the Word of our God stands forever. *(Isaiah 40:8)*

We have seen that picky partakers of the Word and man-made doctrines cause many to miss out on some of God's greatest blessings. Unbelief can stop the very purposes of God from being fulfilled in your life.

… 'Abraham believed God, and it was accounted to him for righteousness.' And he was called the friend of God'
(James 2:23)

God longs to call us friend.

The following scriptures tell some of the wonderful things God did for us. In *Luke 4:18-19* Jesus told those in the synagogue at Nazareth that He was the fulfillment of *Isaiah 61:1, 2* and *Isaiah 49:8, 9:*

> *"The Spirit of the Lord is upon Me, Because He has anointed Me to preach the gospel to the poor; He has sent Me to heal the brokenhearted, To preach deliverance to the captives And recovery of sight to the blind, To set at liberty those who are oppressed, To preach the acceptable year of the Lord."*

Isaiah 53:5 promises: *"...by His stripes we are healed."*

Psalm 103:2-6 reminds us:

> *"Bless the Lord, O my soul, And forget not all His benefits: Who forgives all your iniquities, Who heals all your diseases, Who redeems your life from destruction, Who crowns you with loving kindness and tender mercies, Who satisfies your mouth with good things, So that your youth is renewed like the eagle's. The Lord executes righteousness and justice for all who are oppressed."*

What a wonderful God we serve!

Chapter Eight
Priorities

After our son's death our first priority became mustering strength to get to church regularly. There we were able to learn about God and have the support of other believers. We also learned how to sing praises and worship God. A lifestyle of praise leaves no entryway for hostile elements or anxious thoughts. Praising God allowed peace to replace the heaviness in our hearts. God abides in our praise. Our praise became a powerful spiritual weapon and a source of strength. It helped focus our attention on God. Praise and worship was a pleasurable experience which allowed us to once again feel joy and contentment. It provided a way for us to express our thankfulness to God for all the many ways He was blessing us.

"You will keep him in perfect peace, whose mind is stayed on You, because he trusts in You. Trust in the Lord forever, for in YAH, the Lord, is everlasting strength." Isaiah 26:3

The first several weeks, I found it strange that I could keep my composure during the week, then openly wept as I walked into church. I realize now the presence of God made me weep as He was healing my broken heart. Pastor Lee Jones always extended God's love by greeting us with one of his great big bear hugs.

Other priorities changed. In addition to coming into a personal relationship with Jesus, we recognized in a new way how precious our loved ones are. They are cherished gifts created in God's image, deserving tender love, honor and respect. God puts a high priority on the way we treat our family and will bless us for good stewardship in this area.

Just as the laws of gravity are predictable so are God's commands for the family. It begins in the marriage relationship. *"...let each one of you in particular so **love** his own wife as himself, and let the wife see that she **respects** her husband." Ephesians 5:33* God created in man a need for respect and gave women a craving to be loved. Each of us must put these principles into action with the knowledge that love begets respect and respect begets love.

I have observed great favor on families where a husband and wife set Godly examples of a tender love and respect for one another. The children are blessed observing loving parents and a pattern is set for their success.

God also instructs the husband saying: *"...the Lord has been witness between you and the wife of your youth...she is your companion and your wife by covenant. ...did He not make them one ...why? ...He seeks godly offspring. Therefore take heed to your spirit, and let none deal treacherously with the wife of his youth" (Malachi 2:14-15). I Peter 3:7* promises,*"...husbands, dwell with them with understanding,* *giving honor to the wife…being **heirs** together of the **grace** of life, that **your prayers may not be hindered.***"

And to the wife He says: "*The heart of her husband trusts in her confidently…She comforts, encourages, and does him only good as long as there is life within her*" (*Proverbs 31:11-12 AMP*) and: "*Do not let your beauty be that outward adorning…let it be the hidden person of the heart, with the incorruptible ornament of a gentle and quiet spirit, which is very precious in the sight of God*" (*I Peter: 3-4*).

A special anointing is released by the Holy Spirit for blessing and ministry when a man walks in unity with his wife.

Behold, how good and how pleasant it is for brethren to dwell together in unity! It is like the precious oil upon the head…there the Lord commanded the blessing—Life forevermore. (*Psalm 133:1-3*)

And the charge is very clear for us as children: "*Honor your father and mother, which is the first commandment with promise: that it may be well with you and you may live long on the earth.*" (*Ephesians 6:2-3*).

I recently learned a new lesson through a speaker in Toronto. One day, the Lord revealed to the speaker's wife the subconscious resentment she held against her father. A lot of responsibility had been placed on her at a young age after her mother died. She had often wondered why she hadn't felt deep grief and a sense of loss over his death years earlier. As she repented, it released the pent up grief and pain she held in her heart. Following this, the Lord began to heal some long-standing medical problems. She had worn eyeglasses from age twelve and took medicine for hypothyroidism. Both, which usually get worse with age, began to improve. Her doctors were amazed and decrease her prescriptions each time she returns for checkups. The speaker mentioned how we bring dishonor to our parents even after they are gone by pointing out a fault, being sarcastic, or joking about them. This applied to me with an in-law.

Let no foul or polluting language, nor evil word nor unwholesome or worthless talk [ever] come out of your mouth, but only such [speech] as is good and beneficial to the spiritual progress of others, as is fitting to the need and the occasion, that it may be a blessing and give grace (God's favor) to those who hear it. (*Ephesians 4:29 AMP*)

Our words are powerful. Honor one another in all you say. My dad told us as kids and pretty much lived by this saying: *"If you can't say something nice about someone, then don't say anything."* My aim today is to show honor to my family in all I think or say. This is God's command with the promise that we will live well and long.

Judge not, that you be not judged. For with what judgment you judge, you will be judged; and with the same measure you use, it will be measured back to you. (*Matthew 7:1-2*)

...the Lord does not see as man sees; for man looks at the outward appearance, but the Lord looks at the heart.

(I Samuel 16:7)

And be kind to one another, tenderhearted, forgiving one another, even as God in Christ forgave you.(Ephesians 4:32)

Another extremely important way we bring honor to others is with a joyful spirit. *"God hath anointed thee with the oil of gladness above thy fellows." (Hebrews 1:9 KJV)* And we, too, benefit because our very strength comes from joy.

Do not sorrow, for the joy of the Lord is your strength.

(Nehemiah 8:10)

I will rejoice in the Lord, I will joy in the God of my salvation. The Lord God is my strength...

(Habakkuk 3:18-19)

I can make the choice to be joyful. The Israelites, at one time, faced consequences for not serving God with a joyful and thankful heart after all He had done for them.

*Do all things without complaining and disputing, that you may be blameless and harmless, children of God without fault in the midst of a crooked and perverse generation, among whom you **shine** as lights in the world.*

(Philippians 2:14-15)

49

You or I may be the one person who can change the complexion of a situation or the atmosphere in a room. I like to think of my Uncle Ernie who lit up the room when he walked in. Young and old alike loved him. And he had a knack for narrowing in on the person who needed a lift in their spirit. I recall helping settle my Aunt Bess, his wife, in her hospital room for a minor surgery. My uncle arrived, said hello, and then walked over to the little old lady in the other bed. She looked very sad and lonely and had her covers pulled up to her chin. He said, *"You have beautiful blue eyes, do you mind if I sing you an old Irish melody?"* Her eyes and face lit up as he sang. He might have been the only "light" in her wilderness that day. Joy is a fruit of the spirit and represents an attribute of God that we must show the world. People are drawn to happy joyful folks. They may look at you and say, "I want what you have."

A goal of mine is to make a conscious effort to practice producing good fruit in my spirit. I pray it doesn't take me as many episodes as it did the character Phil Connors in the movie "Ground Hog Day" to get it right. Don't wait as we did for a crisis to line up your priorities in life!

Blessed is everyone who fears the Lord, who walks in His ways...You shall be happy, and it shall be well with you.
(Psalm 128:1-2)

Chapter Nine
Dealing with Grief

Grief is a road that each individual travels in his own way. Healing from a tragedy has many components and every member of my family handled their pain differently.

Our son Lance appeared to have the most difficulty. Initially he was extremely restless, could not sit still or come to terms with him self. He wandered about, had trouble finding direction for his life, and seemed to want to drop out of society. Todd was his kid brother, twenty-one months younger. Lance was the soccer coach the first season Todd's high school had a team. Todd was becoming one of his outstanding players. Each player on the large twenty-one member team was rotated in, even those who had never played soccer before. This helped team spirit as all pulled together. Amazingly they won every game. This relationship had drawn Lance and Todd much closer to each other.

Lance was so angry after the young driver's trial that he wanted to take matters into his own hands. He felt the six-month sentence (which most likely was suspended) plus some financial restitution* was a mere slap on the wrist. He

---

* I mention the following only to show the laxness of society in owning up to responsibility. The young man made only a couple

was ready to dispose of the young man and assured me that no one would ever know. I assured him it would greatly compound matters for us and that it was best to let God handle it. With our encouragement Lance went off to college at DeVry Institute of Technology within six months of Todd's death. He graduated with a B.S. in electronic engineering, which has served him well in this day of computers. Lance first put out pictures of his brother after he was married; his wife Lisa helped him work through much of his pain. In hindsight he would have benefited from being better anchored in the Lord before leaving home. Only through Lance's reviewing this book did I become aware he still needed to forgive the driver. I was able to lead him in a prayer of forgiveness. All of his own family are saved and working on drawing closer to Jesus. Lance and Lisa have five children; Tony, Nicolas, Sarah, William and Matthew Todd.

---

payments of $25 to help with hospital bills. His probation officer called us to say they were dropping this requirement because we had insurance. (We believe forgiveness of the debt should have been up to us). We collected only on our auto insurance (he had none) which paid for the replacement of our car. Kaiser Medical Insurance did not pay for our expenses because Gary was treated at the hospital where I worked. God took care of us and we could not afford to worry about what the young man did or did not do. Neither the plastic surgeon who worked on Gary's face for four hours nor the anesthesiologist who spent ten hours asked us to pay them. It was one of the many blessings we received.

Gary internalized his grief and quietly worked it out. His way of handling the pain was very different from mine. After recovering from his physical wounds, it seemed to me he was back to business as usual. I finally asked him about it, and he said, *"Gail, if you only knew how many dozens of times I have lived the scene over in my mind!"* I never asked again. Although I was not at the trial, Gary had to testify and told me he broke down sobbing when asked by the prosecutor if there was anyone else in his car at the time of the accident. I never saw him cry in my presence. Eventually he said to me, *"When I finally realized there was nothing I could do to change what had happened, I just gave it all up to the Lord."* A noteworthy experience happened much later when we led a Church on the Way home group. Gary expressed his regrets at not verbalizing or demonstratively showing his love to Todd when he was alive. He took the opportunity that evening to tell every person in the room he loved them and physically embraced each one. There wasn't a dry eye in the room as the Holy Spirit ministered the Father's love through Gary.

Aside from church, the highlight of our long days in the weeks and months that followed was our young son Shawn. He was a very sweet, happy and joyful little boy. Our hearts melted every time we looked at him. He had lost Todd, his best buddy and constant companion. He could not understand death at his tender age. Our explanation to Shawn was simply that Todd had gone to heaven. As Lance went off to college, Shawn, three and a half asked, *"Are there schools in heaven?"* Todd was so crazy about Shawn you might have thought *he* was the dad. Before Shawn's birth, Todd, then thirteen, insisted that he get the baby goods out of the attic and that only he set up the crib. He made this statement to me, *"I hope I don't have to wait in the father's waiting room."*

This advice was given us by Dr. James Dobson, providentially in a prayer circle* with us at TCOTW: *"When*

---

* Prayer circles involve three or four people taking hands, sharing a personal prayer request, then praying for one another for about five minutes. Pastor Jack carefully explained them each week and every person was encouraged to get in one. We looked around and made sure new or hesitant people were included. Every church service had a prayer circle without fail at some point during the worship time. When the singing started again it was our cue to finish praying and return to worship. While very intimidating at first, these prayer times became a great blessing to us. Gary and I learned from others how to pray, trust, share needs and receive prayer. We found that every person has some prayer need every week. Not only did we receive personal prayer but we each had an opportunity to minister to others. A spiritual connection was made with others in your prayer circle (unlike a handshake). You could pray, if needed, for those in your circle during the ensuing week and inquire of them the next time paths crossed. We were seated beside different people each week so we always prayed with someone new. If deeper problems were identified, pastors and servants council members were available in the prayer room for more prayer after each service. When someone

Shawn is old enough to comprehend the situation, you, Gary, are to explain the events to him." I do regret I had Shawn in my arms when I was taken to the emergency room to see Gary. You might have thought the nurse who had actually seen Gary's injuries would have warned me. Seeing his dad with his face and knee laid wide open could not have been good for his tender mind. Through the years I pondered what affect this could have had on him. When Shawn was ten he came rushing out from watching a movie at a friend's house and said, *"I can't watch this; the man was in a car accident. But, I know it turns out all right at the end."* I immediately realized what was happening and we all laid hands on him and prayed.

During and after completing his B.A. at Oral Roberts University, Shawn spoke of becoming a doctor. He strongly considered chiropractic medicine because he was sure he didn't want to see blood or perform surgeries. Again I wondered if this was a result of seeing his dad prior to surgery. God directed him elsewhere. Shawn finished law school at Regent University. His going to Regent, but not

---

received the Lord in a prayer circle or in the service (and there was always an invitation) they were escorted to another room staffed by a pastor. He prayed with them, gave them a teaching tape, and a Bible if needed, plus information to help them get started on their walk with God. Some amazing stories came forth from those once "dreaded" prayer circles. They helped unite the body and stretched us to grow spiritually.

necessarily law school, was another desire I had tucked away in my heart and forgotten until this writing. I can recall where I was standing when the seemingly remote possibility leaped into my heart. Shawn was about thirteen years old at the time.

> *Delight yourself also in the Lord and He shall give you the desires of your heart.* (Psalm 37:4)

Today Shawn and his wife Stephanie have three children, Korrynn, Todd, and Sadey. They are faithfully involved in the ministry of their church.

My way of dealing with grief was different from the rest of my family. Talking about the incident and Todd helped me. Initially my mother tried to shield me from phone calls but I soon realized talking was therapeutic. I spoke with difficulty and tears at first; however, I found the more I talked the easier it became. Pastor Lee Jones started me off when I had a pre-funeral interview with him three days after the accident. The first thing he said was, *"Tell me about your son Todd."* It hit me like a ton of bricks and I scrambled to gather my thoughts. Now I can see this was good, as my mind felt so fractured and scattered at the time.

I joined one of the small women's home Bible study/care groups. It proved to be a huge blessing and an important support system. After opening in prayer, we sang praises to usher us into His throne room. Short testimonies were shared. The remaining two-thirds of our time was divided between studying the Word and personal prayer needs. I am grateful to my friend Peggy* who took me under her wing to join the first Bible study/care group at TCOTW. As that group grew and split, I went on to the next. Within a few months I had been in three different groups. At that time we prayed for each woman every day; thus, I quickly came to know thirty women by name. I was blessed to be a part of the last group for many years. The prayer over our families was priceless. We also prayed for the pastor, church and our government leaders. I have a valuable resource in the lifelong prayer partners formed with Maria, Beverly and Raimunda. To this day they remain faithful to pray with me anytime I call. I can honestly say I would not be where I am in my walk with God if not for their knowledge of scriptures and Christ-like input into my life.

* Peggy and Keith Stabe welcomed their 11th grandson in 2006. This birth is a continuing fulfillment of God's promise to them. When their eleven-month-old son Jeffrey died God promised to bless them abundantly. God has given them a grandson for every month that Jeffrey lived. They also have two granddaughters.

Chapter Ten
Fruit

Activities outside the church also helped Gary and me move back into a more wholesome life. I include them so you might be prompted to find things that would be beneficial and encourage you to step out in some way. Our son Todd was full of energy. He loved life and cherished all of our family traditions. He would not be happy to see us sitting around pouting our life away. It would please him to see that the loss of his life was not fruitless. At the memorial service Pastor Lee Jones pointed out Jesus' words: *"Most assuredly, I say to you, unless a grain of wheat falls into the ground and dies, it remains alone; but if it dies, it produces much grain" (John 12:24).* He mentioned the story of Joseph. Joseph told his brothers:

> *"God turned into good what you meant for evil, for He brought me to this high position I have today so that I could save the lives of many people" (Genesis 50:20 TLB).*

In Hebrew the word "meant" is "chashab"--plait (braid), to weave or fabricate. As only God can do, He took our tragedy and intricately wove it into good for His glory.

I found it important for me to stay active rather than isolate myself. Focusing on an event over an extended period of time seems only to magnify the issue. Our loss had the potential to become an idol and crowd out God's redemptive work in the situation. You may find it strange, but Gary and I did not spend much time mourning over Todd's gravesite. We visited only a few times. We believed his spirit was with the Lord. Additionally, considering the fact we'd told Shawn that his brother Todd was in heaven, what kind of witness would it have provided young and impressionable Shawn if we'd spent inordinate visitation beside Todd's grave. I prefer picturing Todd in heaven and smiling when thinking about him. He is most likely having a good time with his quick wit and fulfilling his potential of being a great leader. I am looking forward to the day when we will meet again.

It took some bravery to participate in functions that were emotionally difficult. Here are some examples:

1. We went to see Todd's soccer team win their final game (6-0) which they had dedicated to him. It was bittersweet to watch as Todd had been a key player in the center half position.

2. We left the comfort of our home in California and visited Virginia several weeks after the accident. We gained lifetime friends, received healing, and got to know Jesus better.

3. Just four months after the accident our family took my first division club soccer team, the "Sunhawks," to tour Germany for five weeks. There were 18 sixteen-to-nineteen–year-old boys on the team. For over five years, I had

scouted, recruited, managed and obtained the team's coaches. Without Todd, we didn't want to go but plans had been in motion for a year. Had we not gone, the trip would have been canceled, disappointing our son Lance and all the other boys on my team. It was a memorable trip all hosted by the Germans with the exception of airfare. Adidas provided warm up suits. We stayed in private homes and sports centers and played in the big stadiums of several cities. Our team made U.S. soccer look good by winning every game except the two in Hanover. The Mayor of West Berlin hosted a luncheon for us in the Reichstag, which overlooked the infamous Berlin wall with its 24/7 armed guard towers (a very sobering sight). Gary gave a speech and we exchanged gifts from our Los Angeles mayor and the West Berlin mayor as they are sister cities. After Todd's death, the many hours a week I had spent on soccer, I now spent seeking the Lord.

4. Attending another funeral after Todd's was very draining emotionally but I knew it was another hurdle to cross.

5. Everyday living presented numerous challenges. It was hard to believe Todd was gone. I would wake up in the morning, hoping it was a nightmare; then realize it was not; get in the shower and cry my eyes out. Going to the grocery store, I'd reach for the raisin bran and then remember there was no need to buy Todd's favorite cereal anymore. I was overly sensitive while shopping. It upset me when I saw

parents speaking unkindly to their children or to one another.

6. I literally could not watch Corrie ten Boom's "The Hiding Place," as it was too painful seeing people mistreated. (I subsequently was able to view it, and found much to be gleaned.) I learned that God wants us not only to guard our own eyes and heart but especially those of our children.

Finally, brethren, whatever things are true, whatever things are noble, whatever things are just, whatever things are pure, whatever things are lovely, whatever things are of good report, if there is any virtue and if there is anything praiseworthy—meditate on these things.

(Philippians 4:8)

Carefully screen what you watch and monitor the amount of time you and your children are exposed to movies, TV, computer activities and electronic games. Most lack godly principles and some are downright evil. Set parameters and refer to a wholesome movie guide such as www.movieguide.org if need be. It is easy to allow electronics to become babysitters. Too much time spent on these activities depersonalizes human beings. Beneficial is setting aside one night a week for family time and activities or games without electronics. We were created for fellowship! Sunshine, fresh air and using one's imagination are also essential to wholesome living. Isolation and loneliness are a major problem in society today, and unfortunately, even in many churches.

As parents we may camp outside a store for hours or days to get the latest gadget and schedule far too many extracurricular activities for our children. But do our children see us pursuing time with God and family as vigorously as carnal gain? Our priorities will become theirs. One of our battles here in America is having every kind of distraction to our faith and valuable family time. This takes our focus off God. Living in a society that is moving toward no moral absolutes, it is essential to have the discipline to take time with our children daily to read the Bible, pray and have family devotions. Good seed sown will pay off significantly and lead to success and happiness in our personal lives, and more importantly, in our children's.

7. In the back of my mind I worried no one would come to visit me after all the busyness of the first few weeks. Maybe people would not know what to say or how to handle their own emotions. I worried about being lonely. Our home felt empty. My life went from having two busy teenagers with all their games and extra activities, to one small child at home. We were introduced to new friends at church but we had to make an effort to meet others. *Proverbs 18:24 "A man who has friends must himself be friendly."*

8. Inviting people to dinner was intimidating. However, one of the first activities I found joy and comfort in was

setting a pretty table. It stirred up some creativity in me and my table was often set two days in advance.

9. We participated in two home fellowship groups. It was in those settings where we really got to know people on a more intimate level. We looked forward to each gathering. Eventually we were asked to lead a group. We expressed our concerns to Pastor Lee Jones that it was premature for us with our limited knowledge. He said, *"Yes, but you have big hearts and that's all God needs."* We led a group in our home for three years. It caused us to be stretched and grow spiritually. When we were least prepared it seemed the Lord would show up in a big way touching everyone's heart. As mentioned elsewhere, I joined a women's Bible study. I supposed it would be a little uncomfortable for me since I knew so little scripture. But of course the ladies were very loving and the prayer was extremely helpful. It became a highlight in my week.

10. It was a challenge, but also comforting, to put together a photo/scrapbook of Todd's life. There were little poems he had written and pictures drawn as a young child. We also found letters from girls claiming to be girlfriends (we did not know he had any). I even turned up business cards: **"Four Star Window Washing"** call Todd Stevens (really?). And of course our most prized possession, his precious testimony.

11. Composing a letter about Todd to send to his school took many hours. Just putting my thoughts down on paper was beneficial had the letter never been sent. In subsequent years, I have found it helpful to write down my feelings and

frustrations. I also seek applicable scriptures to quote and stand on in prayer when discouraging thoughts or feelings emerge. Sharing burdens and praying with your mate or a trusted friend is also very good. In nursing school, a visiting professor of psychology carried this lovely quote in his pocket at all times:

"Oh the comfort, the inexpressible comfort of feeling safe with a person having neither to weigh thoughts nor measure words, but pouring them all right out, just as they are, chaff and grain together, certain that a faithful hand will take and sift them, keep what is worth keeping and then with the breath of kindness, blow the rest away..."

Dinah Marie Mulock Craik 1826-1887

Of course, Jesus, whose ears and eyes are open twenty-four hours a day,* is the first one to whom we should turn. One of our Lord's names is *"The Lion of the tribe of Judah."* In my bedroom is a rich pastel oil of a magnificent lion's head and mane. It was painted during a prophetic conference in Pennsylvania. It comforts me because his eyes seem to be looking at me and then I recall this scripture, *"Behold, He who keeps Israel shall neither slumber nor sleep"* (Psalm 121:4). God is always available to help us.

The Lord gave us a beautiful peace that first year. I had a tangible sense of God's presence surrounding me as a cloud of protection. This was especially comforting when I felt uneasy driving or riding in a car. As we sought God, He sorted out our problems and made life simple. Tasks that would normally take two or three weeks to accomplish took a day or a simple telephone call. There was so much grace on us that I started thinking that it might only last one year. Of course this wasn't true but He does expect us to become co-laborers with Him. He carried us for that year. Then, as we began to mature spiritually and learn how to "stand on our own two feet," Jesus expected us to start showing others the grace and love He had showered on us.

Blessed be the God and Father of our Lord Jesus Christ, the Father of mercies and God of all comfort, who comforts us in all our tribulation, that we may be able to comfort those who are in any trouble, with the comfort with which we ourselves are comforted by God. (2 Corinthians 1:3-4)

A very different dynamic emerges when the presence of God is not invited into a crisis. I witnessed this with my good friend who lost her sixteen-year-old son to leukemia three months after Todd died. In trying to witness to her, I agreed to go with her to a community sponsored group for grieving parents. Ten to twelve families were represented around a very large oval table. One by one we shared our stories. Most of the people could hardly speak without breaking down or sobbing. I took an opportunity to ask how long it had been since they lost their children. I was astonished to learn that for most it had been two to twelve years prior. Their lives seemed to be on hold as though the loss had happened last week; there was no relief in sight. My friend also shared with me that her grandmother lost a five-year-old child and the rest of her life seemingly revolved around the incident. Imagine the toll that would take on a person and all those around them. I believe there is sorrow so deep that only with God's help can we be fully restored.

While in Germany with the soccer team, I met a man that had lost a child within the previous two years. As I began sharing about the loss of our son, he confided to me that he had never spoken to anyone about the death of his son. He and his wife isolated themselves from people and social activities. They closed the window shades in their home and removed all his pictures. He was so relieved to have someone to talk to about the loss of their child. I am very thankful we turned to God. He helped us take steps forward.

Chapter Eleven
Rainbowitis

My husband and I were blessed to have three sons, Lance, Todd, and Shawn. Still, deep in my heart, I also longed for a daughter. In fact, for fifteen years I had saved a baby girl's layette which had been given to me. I did not dwell on this all the time, but my eyes were open to possibilities. At work I asked the obstetrical doctors to be on the look out for a red-headed baby girl. As we investigated adoption we found very few babies available at that time. If you were over forty or had children of your own, you did not qualify. Gary and I prayed about it and put it on the back burner.

The Church on the Way had a tradition of having each person write a letter to the Lord on New Year's Eve. They provided paper, envelope and a time to write during the service. Several months later, those letters were mailed back to us. Included in my letter of December 31, 1982 was the following, *"Dear Lord Jesus, Let your light shine thru me, reaching, touching others in all I say or do... Add an Anna girl to our family Lord if it would glorify you—a happy, healthy baby girl, naturally or through adoption—as wonderful a blessing to us as Shawn has been."* On March 1, 1983 the letter was mailed back. I reread my commitments to the Lord, my prayer requests, and checked off answered prayers. I also made note of the "in progress requests" and filed the letter in my dresser drawer. On occasion, I still love to pull out and reread those letters.

Now in addition to all the other ways the Lord was blessing, He encouraged me with signs in the form of rainbows as a reassurance of His presence in our midst. My heart was greatly moved by these special touches.

Like the appearance of a rainbow in a cloud on a rainy day, so was the appearance of the brightness all around it. This was the appearance of the likeness of the glory of the Lord.
(Ezekiel 1:28)

The rainbow is a sign of God's everlasting covenant relationship with man. It represents divine promise and possibility to all who come into a relationship with God. Here are the events that first led my attention to rainbows.

October 30, 1983. While lifting my hands to praise the Lord, I received a vision of rays of sun coming into the palms of my hands and the word, *"Your praises establish direct contact with God and He is able to pour His Holy Spirit through you to minister to others."*

October 31, 1983. We had been looking for property and one day the name *"Rainbow Ranch"* came to mind. So I inquired of the Lord. *"Ranch, does that mean acreage?"* His answer, *"Rainbow Ranch shall be wherever My Glory* *dwells. It will be wherever you are because My Glory dwells in you."*

November 1, 1983. A note came in the mail from the very area where we had been looking for property with a rainbow on it. That same evening Gary called me outside to see an unusual beautiful double rainbow. The next day a picture of it was on the front page of the newspaper.

November 3, 1983. While sitting in my powder room in the exact spot I'd been many times over the previous eighteen years, a perfect rainbow, each color distinct, came across the page I was reading and down onto my hand. My heart leaped. I began praising the Lord and shouting *"Hallelujah."* Immediately, two things came to mind. I recalled the sun ray vision of October 30th and I knew the Lord had touched me saying, *"I have not forgotten you and I am going to fulfill the promises I have given to you and Gary."*

November 6, 1983. In the Sunday evening service, Pastor John Wilkens delivered the word of prophesy he had received when he saw the same double rainbow we had seen November 1st. Essentially it said, "double blessings are coming to the congregation through the women of the church."

November 14, 1983. Gary was dancing around the kitchen teasing me about rainbows as he spots three rainbows on the sink. The one in the middle had a cross in it with the rainbow going down around the sides of the cross.

November 27, 1983. During "Rainbow Night" (name given TCOTW home group meetings) at our home we asked for prayer explaining that we had been going through several months of travailing and felt it was time for the "*birthing process*" to take place. We were referring to Gary's career and not a physical birth.

November 29, 1983. Gary was home for lunch (very unusual) and my dearest Aunt Bess and Uncle Ernie were visiting. A phone call came in from the mother of another student in Shawn's first grade class at Granada Hills Baptist School. She said, "*I don't know how to ask you this or what you are going to say, but would you and Gary be interested in six-month-old twin girls?*" She said it took me three seconds to answer "*Yes!*" I had two questions for her. "*How many other people are lined up for them?*" She could find no one else willing to take them after making numerous phone calls. She was unable to keep them herself as she and her husband had three young boys. Her church called and she had been kind enough to temporarily take the twins and their half sister. This was to prevent them from going into county foster care. At the time, Los Angeles County had a rule you could only have one foster child at a time in your home under one year old even if they were twins. The second question was, "*When can we have them?*" Her answer, "*I'll be over in an hour.*"

Gary and I prayed and I asked the Lord to give me a word in the Scriptures. Beside myself with excitement, I opened my Bible and just started reading. In this order, I read:

"The sun shall no longer be your light by day, Nor for brightness shall the moon give light to you; But the Lord will be to you an everlasting light, And your God your glory. Your sun shall no longer go down, nor shall your moon withdraw itself; For the Lord will be your everlasting light, and **the days of your mourning shall be ended**" (Isaiah 60:19, 20).

These Words so ministered to me, I went to the beginning of the chapter:

"Arise, shine; for your light has come! And the glory of the Lord is risen upon you... **Your sons shall come from afar, and your daughters shall be nursed at your side. Then you shall see and become radiant**, *and your heart shall swell with joy"* (Isaiah 60:1, 4, 5).

Former neighbors of the twin's grandmother, Lois and Bob Keefer, identified the dire circumstances of the family. The grandmother was caring for her daughter's five children ages six months to thirteen years with no beds, cribs, telephone or car. She was about to be evicted from her adult-only HUD apartment for which she had waited a long time to acquire. Lois called her church to find someone to care for the children in lieu of them being placed in foster care. The children's mother and her boyfriend, we were told, were living out of the back of a Ranchero truck. We met with the grandmother who agreed to allow us to care for the twins "*temporarily*" in the absence of her daughter. As the months went by, we believed that permanent placement was in order. Eventually we challenged the grandmother to think about what she thought was best for the twins. We told her we would not fight with their family to keep them. We wanted them to want us to raise them. However we did ask the Lord to prepare the hearts of each member of their family to release them to us.

Be specific when you pray as the Lord delights in giving you the desires of your heart. I asked for an Anna and with tongue in cheek, a redhead. I asked for one child but God gave us two—a double blessing. They were delivered at Northridge Hospital, the very place Todd had been taken after the accident. Write your dreams and find a scripture to go with them because the Word of God not only breathes life into our prayers but also gives them wings. Exercise your faith by believing God's Word, be obedient and committed to your vision or dream. Steward it in your heart, allow it to incubate and in due time your God-given dreams will come to fruition.

Trust in the Lord, and do good; dwell in the land, and feed on His faithfulness. Delight yourself also in the Lord and He shall give you the desires of your heart. Commit your way to the Lord, trust also in Him, and He shall bring it to pass. He shall bring forth your righteousness as the light, and your justice as the noonday. Rest in the Lord, and wait patiently for Him... Cease from anger, and forsake wrath; do not fret, it only causes harm. (Psalm 37:3-8)

December 4, 1983. My heart is so full it is bursting with joy. As I sat at church during the evening Christmas program I began talking to the Lord. *"Lord what is to be the outcome with these babies?"* He responded, *"Receive them; they are a gift from Me."* I awoke in the night and asked the same question. Again I heard, *"Receive them; they are a gift from Me."* Tears filled my eyes. It was hard to believe and I found myself guarding my heart. The comments of other people didn't help. *"Watch out, you may get hurt." "Why don't you give them to someone who has no children?" "Do you know how old you and Gary will be when they graduate from high school?"* All I could say was, *"God gave them to us."*

I set My rainbow in the cloud, and it shall be for the sign of the covenant between Me and the earth. And I will remember My covenant which is between Me and you and every living creature of all flesh. (Genesis 9:13, 15)

Isaiah 54:9-10 says:

> "...like the waters of Noah... I have sworn that I would not be angry with you, nor rebuke you. For the mountains shall depart and the hills be removed, but My kindness shall not depart from you, nor shall my covenant of peace be removed, says the Lord, who has mercy on you."

Chapter Twelve
The Birthday

*M*onths went by and we were all wrapped up in "our" twins. Anna Gabrielle means "grace, mercy or prayer and God is my strength" and Aimee Elizabeth, "beloved and consecrated to God." Although no legal work had begun, Gary and I actively sought counsel from many sources, even attorneys. Nobody knew how to advise us in such unusual circumstances. We were confused as to how to proceed because, in spite of our concentrated efforts, we had been unable to make contact with the mother.

On March 7, 1984 I petitioned the Lord in a very difficult prayer, *"Dear Lord God, If Gary and I are not the ones with the wisdom to raise these babies to be a blessing to You and to our family, especially when they reach the teenage years, then please take them from us now. In Jesus' name."* I was feeling inadequate and fearful particularly of the adolescent years.

The very next day I suddenly recalled several months earlier I had put a date on a scripture and even made note of it in the front of my Bible. It really caught my attention as it just seemed to apply to Gary and me. My thought was that it pertained to plans we had to purchase land. Little did I know its significance until that day.

*Enlarge the place of your tent, and let them stretch out the curtains of your dwellings; do not spare; lengthen your cords, and strengthen your stakes. For **you shall expand to the right and to the left**, and your descendants will inherit the nations, and make the desolate cities inhabited. **Do not fear, for you will not be ashamed; nor be disgraced, for you will not be put to shame.*** (Isaiah 54:2-4)

It was a direct answer to my prayer of the day before! I then read the preceding verse which added further confirmation:

"...Break forth into singing, and cry aloud, you who have not travailed with child! For more are the children of the desolate than the children of the married woman, says the Lord" (Isaiah 54:1).

If there had been any doubt that the Lord was intimately involved in our having the twins, that doubt was completely dispelled when I discovered I had dated it on May 3rd, 1983, the very day of Anna and Aimee's birth. We had no knowledge of their existence until November 29, 1983, the day I got the telephone call when they were six months old. Awesome! Another shout: ***"Hallelujah!"*** There was no question now that we were in the Lord's plan, so we waited on Him for direction. It was all to happen in His perfect timing. God was preparing the hearts of the birth family. All visited our home at various times.

I would be remiss, however, in not confessing to a few anxious moments. One evening a police officer called our house. *"I have a woman at the police station who claims you have her children."* My heart started pounding as I responded, *"Yes, we are caring for them."* He then asked if there were legal proceedings and I told him plans were being formulated. His reply, *"I think I recognize her from being here on other occasions. Thank you."* Not only did their birth mother know where we lived, she could have picked them up at anytime because we had no legal premise to care for them.

On the twin's first birthday the birth mother with a new boyfriend appeared unannounced at our door. This was the first time I had ever seen or spoken with her. It was the only time she ever came to our home, despite all our efforts. When they arrived Gary was in the backyard. *"Oh my!"* I thought. To say I was a little frightened as I tried to talk to them on the porch would be an understatement. The twins' mother asked, *"Aren't you going to invite us in?"* I swallowed hard. *"Yes, of course, please come in."* Everything in me wanted to run and get Gary but I did not want to leave the babies. The mother held each little girl, then told me she tried little "tricks" to see if they remembered her, but they did not. She gave them each a stuffed toy dog which they both still have. I pressed her to see what her plans were for the twins. When she told me I didn't have to worry, I asked her if she would meet with a social worker to sign papers. She agreed but vanished the day we were to go to the social worker. As a reminder, I had called her one week, a day and then an hour before we were to pick her up. At this point, we were back to square one.

The Lord continued to encourage us with scripture or a rainbow just when we needed it most. One day I'd gone to pick Shawn up from school. I opened the car door to call to him and lying at my feet was a large empty envelope with a big rainbow stretched across it. I said, *"Thank you Lord."* It was the precise pick-me-up I needed.

On Anna and Aimee's first birthday a card arrived from a friend who knew nothing of our rainbow signs. It pictured two little angelic girls with different colored hair (Anna is a brunette and Aimee a redhead) sliding down a rainbow with the words "Heavens Above." It was as though the Lord was saying, *"I'm still with you."* No legal work had begun. Seven days after the twins' first birthday their natural grandmother and aunt told us they wanted us to adopt the twins. This was a complete turnaround from the statements they made the day we first received the girls.

A man's heart plans his way, but the Lord directs his steps.   *(Proverbs 16:9)*

Chapter Thirteen
Full Redemption

On October 31, 1984 we had our first interview with the Department of Adoptions. The night before, our eight-year-old son Shawn, came home from a party and said, *"Here is a gift for you, Mom."* It was a note pad picturing two little girls with different color hair. They were in a cart being pulled across the sky by a horse with a rainbow coming out of its saddle. The girls were sprinkling rainbow dust over a church with a bell tower (like the TCOTW prayer chapel). The back of the note pad showed them floating free; holding five balloons (our five children?) and one balloon had a rainbow extending from it (Todd?). Silly, you might say, but I imagine God speaks encouragement to each of us in different ways and His timing is perfect.

The adoption process took two years. The court system assigned three separate attorneys: one represented the birth mother, a second the assumed father, and a third, the presumed father. The "fathers" were both incarcerated at the time. At our first meeting with the judge, the attorneys for the birth mother and the presumed father claimed their clients wanted to fight for the children. After mulling this over for a few days, I was a little bit discouraged. One night, when I arrived home from work about 11:30 p.m., I told the Lord I didn't want to go to bed until I had a scripture to stand on. I was very tired. I opened my Bible and this is what I read: *"Return to the stronghold, you prisoners of hope. Even today I declare that **I will restore double to you**"* *(Zechariah 9:12)*.

I love the way the Word of God touches my spirit. I had no doubt He held the final answer.

The crowning moment came the day before the final court date. As I walked into the Christian bookstore at church my eye immediately caught sight of a picture with, surprise, a rainbow on it. On it was written: *"We know that all things work together for good to those who love God, to those who are the called according to His purpose"* *(Romans 8:28)*. As previously stated, this very scripture was read at Todd's memorial service and was a portion of the scripture on which his testimony was based. At that moment I knew the Lord had brought us full circle to a place of redemption. God indeed had given us *'double for our mourning.'*

I went in peace to the court the next day. However, the drama of five attorneys and a judge who would rule was very real. We did not know if the girls' birth mother would appear. Some thirty minutes late, she did arrive, spoke to the attorneys and took her oath before God. *"Yes I want Gary and Gail Stevens to raise the twins."* Case closed. Praises be to God!!!

Our 25th wedding anniversary photo

Chapter Fourteen
God's Provision

God is called Yahweh Yireh, *"The-Lord-Will-Provide"* in *Genesis 22:14.* He cares for our children–actually His children–more than we do and will provide supernaturally for their needs. When planning a family, it is good to remember this. When God created man, His first command to him is recorded in *Genesis 1:28: "God blessed them, and God said to them, 'Be fruitful and multiply; fill the earth and subdue it; have dominion over...every living thing...'"* God wants Christian families to trust Him for their children. How can we take dominion and fill the earth if we plan our families while worrying about cost, convenience, and believing the myth that the earth is overpopulated? We limit God.

> *Behold, children are a heritage from the Lord, the fruit of the womb is His reward. Like arrows in the hand of a warrior, so are the children of one's youth. Happy is the man who has his quiver full of them.*   *(Psalm 127:3-5)*

> *Blessings on all who reverence and trust the Lord—on all who obey Him! Their reward shall be prosperity and happiness. Your wife shall be contented in your home. And look at all those children! There they sit around the dinner table as vigorous and healthy as young olive trees. That is*

God's reward to those who reverence and trust Him. May the Lord continually bless you with heaven's blessings as well as with human joys. May you live to enjoy your grandchildren! And may God bless Israel!

(Psalm 128:1-6 TLB)

In my parents' generation, families of ten to twelve children were common in the U.S. My dad and Gary's dad were each one of ten children and his mom, one of eleven. I was one of six children and at that time we were considered a very large family. Children in the United States are currently being born at the rate of 2.11 per woman. Great numbers have been lost to abortion. Canada, Japan and many other countries are already below the population replacement rate while the followers of Islam* are having five, six or more children per woman.

At the time we received Anna and Aimee, Gary was without a paying job, and about to start a brand new law practice. We had $80 in our bank account. I scaled down to work part-time evenings so I could be home as much as possible. Gary took over when he came home. I truly wish I had followed the desire of my heart, trusted God and stayed home fulltime not only with the girls but with all our children. My husband and I didn't complete our college educations until after we were married and had two young children. We

---

*See: "America Alone" by Mark Steyn; 2006, Regnery

learned the hard way; it's much wiser to finish your education before you have children.

There is a rich element of love, sensitivity and stability only imparted by a father and a mother. Children need fathers to: *"...rear them [tenderly] in the training and discipline and the counsel and admonition of the Lord"* *(Ephesians 6:4 AMP)*. And children need a mother who: *"opens her mouth in skillful and Godly wisdom, and on her tongue is the law of kindness [giving counsel and instruction]. She looks well to how things go in her household, and the bread of idleness (gossip, discontent, and self-pity) she will not eat. Her children rise up and call her blessed [happy, fortunate, and to be envied]; and her husband boasts of and praises her"* *(Proverbs 31:26-28 AMP)*.

Cherish every moment with your children and grandchildren. They are your heritage from the Lord. Make it a priority to have fun and spend lots of time continually teaching your children about the Lord.

You shall love the Lord your God with all your heart, with all your soul, and with all your strength. And these words which I command you today shall be in your heart. You shall teach them diligently to your children, and shall talk of them when you sit in your house, when you walk by the way, when you lie down, and when you rise up. *(Deuteronomy 6:5-7)*

The payoff is enormous. Not only will they bless you in your old age, you will have the opportunity to set the stage for generations to come. My advice, depend on God as you start your families and He will provide supernaturally even if your situation looks bleak.

Mothers didn't work outside the home a few generations ago. Parents, grandparents and extended family all lived in close proximity. The older men and women helped the younger ones. *Psalm 68:6* tells us *"God sets the solitary in families..."* Why? God provided and intends for family to be a tremendous blessing and a support system throughout our lives. Grandparent, grandchild, aunt and uncle relationships add a very special dimension to each life. Today many families are scattered. Children go off to college all over the States and overseas. Many end up marrying and living far away from their family. Without God in our schools since the 1960's, textbooks and teaching have become godless and liberal. Traditional Christian family values are not reinforced. Today there is a high divorce rate and over half the children in the U.S. are being raised without a father. The breakdown in the family support system creates an anchorless society. A great need in the church today is for mature fathers and mothers in the faith to provide nurturing discipleship for new believers and the younger generation. God sovereignly placed Anna and Aimee in our family to bless both us and them.

God provided all that the girls needed through various people. We were given two of every piece of child equipment, plus clothing and food. The church graciously sent $500 that first month. As the girls grew this pattern continued. When they outgrew their cribs, we were blessed by my friend, Char, who happened to have a Thomasville twin bedroom set she graciously gave us. My neighbor had a friend with a daughter one year older than the girls. This dear lady purchased more clothes for one child than I could use for two. She offered me beautiful expensive dresses that cost $35 or more for $4 a piece. They looked brand new. I purchased a complete wardrobe for $100 for both Anna and Aimee two years in a row.

We were very thankful to the Lord as He continued to provide and bless our family in many creative ways. This has included supernaturally helping us find our homes. Nothing is too difficult for Him!

Trust in the Lord with all your heart, and lean not on your own understanding. In all your ways acknowledge Him, and He shall direct your paths.   *(Proverbs 3:5-6)*

Chapter Fifteen
Blessings

*R*emember the prophecy of "double blessings coming through the women of the church?" The same month we received our twin daughters, two more sets of twin girls were born in the church. One set was Pastor Jack Hayford's granddaughters. The other pair was born to Gabi and Debbie Boone Ferrar. A couple of years later Marie and Ben Crouch (brother of musician Andre Crouch) came to us at church. *"See what you started?"* They had just been given an opportunity to adopt twin girls. This was after already adopting two young girls. Ben and Marie had raised their own children when they decided one way they might serve the Lord was by taking in foster children. Marie pictured herself sitting in a rocking chair pouring love on *"an ugly"* little unwanted child. She was joyfully laughing as she told me the story of how the Lord placed two strikingly gorgeous little girls with them and now the beautiful twins. The nursery workers told us there was an unusual increase in the number of sets of twins and we noticed more individual adoptions as well.

The Lord did help us build Rainbow Ranch. It was built on six acres of land in avocado/lemon/horse country. We had a commanding 180-degree view of the Santa Rosa Valley, the mountains, and cities all the way to the Pacific

Ocean fourteen miles away. The Channel Islands were also within our scenic panorama. Almost daily we enjoyed spectacular sunsets that declared the magnificence of God's creation. Even the children would run, look, and then bid us to come. We lived there for seven years until Gary's job took us to Northern California. And yes, I have a picture of our home with a rainbow over it! Most weekends we also enjoyed rainbow colored hot air balloons floating so close over our home we could speak to the passengers. One even landed on our property because they were running out of daylight.

Recently one of Anna and Aimee's natural siblings, a half sister, found them via the internet. She updated them on their biological family members. Aimee sent this message for her to relay to their birth mother. *"I can't thank you enough for giving us to my parents. Anna and I have had an amazingly blessed life growing up and couldn't have asked for a better family."* I pray this blessed her.

It was very fulfilling watching our children develop over the ensuing years. We have many fond memories. I'd like to share a few of them.

An explanation is frequently given for a photo on the front cover of a book. The picture of the twins on the cover of this book has a cute story to go with it. When six years old, Aimee (left) and Anna (right) were invited to a very fancy birthday party. All the trimmings were provided for them to design and decorate the hats they are wearing. After donning their beautiful new hats, they were invited to the parlor for a tea party. The father, who was a highly respected physician, dressed up in a tuxedo to decant the hot apple cider. He looked and played his part, complete with a towel over his arm to catch drips. When he came to pour for Aimee, she looked up, and innocently asked, *"What's your name?"* He answered, *"I am the butler!"* To which she responded, *"May I call you 'Butt' for short?"*

When the girls were four years old, my Uncle Ernie died. He was ninety-two years old and a favorite of everybody in the family. Our many relatives had gathered and were seated waiting for the funeral to begin. The room was very quiet and everyone was extremely somber. Aimee and Anna sat a couple of rows ahead of us on the laps of two of my elderly aunts. The girls looked toward the open casket that held Uncle Ernie. Then they looked at each other and Anna said in a rather loud voice, *"Isn't someone going to give Uncle Ernie his cane so he can get up out of that box?"* Laughter erupted—exactly what Uncle Ernie, the jokester, would have wanted at his funeral.

One day I saw the girls and our grandsons, Tony and Nicolas, dancing around the yard. They came running inside and announced, *"We were dancing with the angels."* The girls were about ten years old at the time. Anna composed this piece about angels and Aimee typed it.

ANGELS

"I love angels. They are very neat, and pretty. I will tell you a secret. All angels wear robes. Angels can be seen in your dreams. There are many kinds of angels, comforting angels and protecting angels. Angels are very delicate people. They live in Heaven with God. If you ask them to come and protect you, they will. I hope you have learned something about angels." *Anna Stevens*

Take heed that you do not despise one of these little ones, for I say to you that in heaven their angels always see the face of My Father who is in heaven. *(Matthew 18:10)*

Todd and Lance were twelve and fourteen when, without permission, they took their bikes one Sunday morning and rode up and down a large mound of dirt known as Cherry Hill. Lance called to tell me Todd had an accident on his bike. He said, *"Mom, please, I don't want you to worry, Todd is fine. Just a couple of his front teeth are missing."* We found one tooth quickly and I rushed him to the dentist. Gary, Lance and a couple of the boys' friends were left to find the second tooth. A $10 reward was offered. After a bit of time had gone by, I told the dentist, *"My husband has a hard time finding things. Do you mind if I leave Todd here to go look myself?"* Thank goodness, I found the tooth. The dentist was able to put them back in Todd's mouth. Todd also had a mild concussion. (Of course we weren't laughing at the time). As a result, Todd later required orthodontic work at the University of California at Los Angeles, which was in process at the time of the accident. This had motivated him to want to become an orthodontist.

At five years old, Shawn worked hard to memorize a bible verse every week. He found it difficult to recite them in class because the teacher was so stern. He said she never smiled when she looked at him. I told him to ask Jesus to help him whenever he had trouble. He looked at me and said, *"I can't talk out loud* (in class) *to ask Him; I know, I'll say it through my nose."*

❖ Note: This is the one exercise I believe most helped develop Shawn's mind and spirit. Memorizing a weekly scripture was required of all K-6th graders at Granada Hills Baptist School. We worked on it throughout the week. It was also very good for me as I learned with him. In the first grade he was required to memorize the entire Christmas story from Luke. A full typewritten page, it was a ginormous task for a six year old. In an effort to help, I had him draw a series of pictures. Inch upon inch we worked our way through the mountain of verses. He finally mastered it and could recite it for the next few years.

It would be brilliant to have a verse committed to memory from each of the sixty-six books of the Bible! An arsenal! So I have composed a list of choice verses for those who would like to tackle this individually or as a family.*

Gary was praying for an angel to be assigned to protect our car while driving home from church one night. Shawn, then six years old, said, *"Hold it Dad, don't ask for one for me 'cause I already have my own guardian angel. Look out, there are thousands of angels, don't you see them?"*

Gary did see angels in our church recently. My husband is intellectual, a man of few words, true as the day, and not drawn to emotional displays. He and others were being prayed for in several small groups at the front of the church. As he opened his eyes and glanced around he saw angels swirling around every group where people were in prayer. He knew in his heart they were angels because of the radiance of their faces. Several youth and others in our church have seen varying kinds of angels. These special touches help boost our faith in the spiritual realm. Recently, while our pastor was reading a scripture, Victoria, age fourteen, witnessed two angels in the pulpit area of the church. One angel had a basket of fabric and the other held a basket of fruit. When she told me about it, my thought was *"God can take the events in the fabric of our lives and produce fruit from it."*

---

* *Memory Verses* on page 129.

When Shawn was seven years old we were out driving around town doing chores. For some inexplicable reason, Gary was impatient with other drivers that day. We pulled into a gas station and Shawn said, *"Dad, you have a weed growing out of your heart. Jesus is like a flower, the devil is like a weed. You need love instead of hate. Love is Jesus, hate is from the devil. When you don't say nice things, you have weeds growing inside you and when you say nice things you have flowers growing inside you."* Wow! Praise God for the exhortation our children can bring.

Addendum:

Late in the writing of this book, I added *I Kings 17:21-22* to the memory verse list wanting people to know our authority in scriptures. Shortly after and without precedent, a series of four events happened to my computer. It went crazy and crashed—ultimately deleting the file. Several days of work were required to update a previously saved document. On August 1, 2007, I mumbled, *"Like it or not devil, I am going to put I Kings back in."* Two days later our eighteen month old grandson, Nathaniel, drowned in our 540 acre community lake.

His parents, Anna and Kevin, were loading their car to leave for the weekend when Nathaniel suddenly disappeared. It happened so fast their first thought was 'kidnap' and security was called. Running in opposite directions they frantically searched for ten minutes. Anna went left to the beach a few doors down the street, Kevin went across the street to hunt around and behind the houses lining the lake across from their home. We believe Kevin was "divinely" directed to look for a third time in the exact location where he was to find Nathaniel face down, blue/purple and lifeless. He was about eight feet out in the water between two docks. With cries of utter anguish, Kevin rushed Nathaniel up the driveway and immediately started CPR. Anna joined in giving puffs of air. The three security guards who did not know CPR called for a rescue squad and stood by. Clay Jones, the Captain of security, who witnessed the rescue said, *"The baby was gone, blue as blue can get, lifeless as a rag doll. It sent chills through my body."* When Kevin heard gurgling sounds he picked Nathaniel up and said, *"Thank you Jesus, thank you Jesus."*

Within thirty seconds the rescue squad arrived as they were just coming in the gate from another call. Nathaniel was placed in the ambulance, given oxygen and an IV started. Mrs. Gwen Mallman, one of the rescue team members, said this was made much easier because he was not responsive. His general color was poor, extremities bluish, lungs sounded sponge-like, and he remained unresponsive even to his mother's voice as the ambulance left.

At this point I received the call from our daughter Anna. My husband and I were in North Carolina after the birth of

Sadey, our fourth granddaughter, *I Kings 17:21-22* came to mind as we all prayed crying out to God and putting this very scripture into action: *"And he stretched himself out on the child three times, and cried out to the Lord, and said, O Lord My God, I pray, let this child's soul come back to him. Then the Lord heard the voice of Elijah; and the soul of the child came back to him, and he revived."*

I then called Brenda, a prayer warrior friend, who prayed with me. She called Ann, our church Administrative Assistant, who called the church members into prayer. Two large ministries with prayer help-lines also prayed with us and activated others into urgent prayer. Prayer warrior friends across the nation were called into immediate intercessory prayer on our behalf.

Meanwhile, Nathaniel was airlifted by helicopter to a major trauma center in Fairfax, Virginia. One of the men on the rescue squad was so distraught, he went home and cried all afternoon. Anna and Kevin with their one month old baby, Abigail, started north by car for the hospital. Kevin's father worked close by and was first to arrive at the hospital. Shortly after Nathaniel arrived he sent word, *"There is no brain damage!"* "Hallelujah!!!" To God be the glory.

Nathaniel had petechiae (minute hemorrhages) on his skin and in the whites of his eyes which cleared in a few days. He was perfectly restored. He has no fear of the water, and is more affectionate than ever. Puckering up like a fish he frequently comes to plant a kiss right on your lips.

A week later, Nathaniel was sitting quietly in church next to us. Our pastor was playing the keyboard and teaching us a new song he'd written. *"You give strength in the battle."* Nathaniel started clapping and said, *"Yeeaah!"* *"You give strength every hour;"* another clap, clap, clap and *"Yeeaah!"* *"You give strength for the future;"* clap, clap, clap, *"Yeeaah!"* All in the congregation were quiet except for the precious sounds of eighteen month old Nathaniel. I was privately thanking God as it had been prophesied Nathaniel would be "a mighty warrior of God." He seemed to have been responding to the words.

The Lord knows the plans he has for our children before they are born. In January of 2006 while Nathaniel was still in-utero, Amy Bopp (our Pastor's daughter), prophesied over him: *"Anna, the Lord wants you to know your baby is going to be really healthy and every one who sees him is going to know he is a blessing. They will say, 'Wow, he is a blessing to me.' The enemy might try to rob him from you because the destiny your child has is great in the Lord. It's such a special thing and that's why, not only is he going to be known as a blessing, but he is going to be known as a person of God, a mighty warrior of God. There is such a destiny for him and the enemy might try to rob that. Just be careful, just prepare for that."* My response was, *"that's already happened."* Little did I know.

I was referring to an incident a few weeks before this prophesy. Anna couldn't feel movement of her baby (as yet unnamed). She hurried to the doctor's office. When the doctor and nurses couldn't get a response she was rushed to the hospital. The neonatologist and nurses pushed and prodded and sent shock waves to the baby—no response. Prayers started going up. Slowly he started to move. Then the ultrasound technician said, *"Look, he just reached up and kissed your placenta."* A sign to us that God had indeed touched him.

Although we prayed for this baby, I had tucked away the cassette tapes with Amy Bopp's prophesy and others to show him later in life. In hind sight we wish we had been more diligent in our attention and prayers. Nathaniel also had a very difficult Cesarean delivery and additionally received some of the general anesthetic. He was born blue, limp and not breathing, necessitating resuscitation.

Nathaniel's name means "a gift of God." I decree in Jesus name that Nathaniel **shall** live out the full measure of his days and become a mighty warrior for the Lord. Nathaniel is now twenty-one months old. My husband and I watched as his mother was teaching him to say "hallelujah" and raise his arms. She then asked him to say "praise God." Without example, (Anna only looked directly at him), he raised one arm with his hand palm up, looked straight up and said, "praise God" in a very reverent way. He repeated the same scenario with "praise Jesus." One time when we weren't present Anna said he looked up extending his hand and said "Papa." Recently he was laying on the bed gazing up and said a prolonged, "Wowww," as though he was seeing into the supernatural. These incidents touched our hearts as it appears Nathaniel had a personal encounter.

We must be ever mindful of these scriptures:

And let us not grow weary while doing good, for in due season we shall reap if we do not lose heart. (Galatians 6:9)

...The effective, fervent prayer of a righteous man avails much.   (James 5:16)

One day we may know how many times God intervened on our behalf. Thank you Lord for attending to our prayers.

Chapter Sixteen
Looking Ahead

Although the final chapters of our exciting spiritual journey are yet to come. Gary and I continue to marvel at God's blessings. We are looking ahead with great anticipation and excitement.

I am proud of each and every member of my family, in particular because they all know Jesus. As *3 John 4* relates, *"I have no greater joy than to hear that my children walk in truth."* Anna and Kevin with their children Nathaniel and Abigail, and Aimee with her fiancé Adam, attend church regularly with us. I can't tell you how it blesses Gary's and my heart to have our children and grandchildren sitting beside us in church. Both girls finished two years at Bible colleges: Anna at Texas Bible Institute and Aimee at Life East Bible College. In addition Aimee was "pinned" with my nursing school pin as she completed her own nursing degree at Germanna Community College.

While each one of us has had bumps along the path, I praise God that He looks directly at our heart and sees us as His bride in preparation for His return. I am certain as we follow His ways He will faithfully walk with us to finish the race with flying colors.

I am thankful God does not show partiality by sizing us

up and deciding whether we are fit to be his friend or servant. His desire is for every single one of us to come to Him just as we are and experience the abundance of His love. We don't have to be perfect before we come; the Holy Spirit will help us grow. As Todd so aptly stated in his testimony, *"Even though I have made many mistakes and sins in the past, I am not condemned. No one can condemn me from God's grace."* We should all say a hearty "Amen!" God has uniquely gifted each one of us for a tailor-made place in His ministry. It is our job as the church to take time to show the Father's love through nurture, discipleship, encouragement, and providing opportunity for the treasures resident in each precious saint to be unwrapped. We must then mobilize them in service to others. Our slogan should be; "Every member a minister," as every believer is called to be a royal priest in the kingdom of God.

I believe to facilitate a more biblical church model we must return to a family covenant and abandon the business or orphanage-like atmosphere seen in many churches. Each person desires a sense of security, belonging, and wants to know that they are appreciated and vital to the body. The church must operate like a loving family. Unity through restoration of individuals, families and generations will allow God's anointing to flow and break the curse of fatherlessness in the land. Great is the need for the more mature in faith to be available to the younger generation and new believers as spiritual mothers and fathers.

104

Both strong biological and church families are the backbone of a healthy nation. In *Acts 2:17-19* God relates that in the last days His Spirit is going to be poured out on individuals who are His servants—young and old. It's an exciting time in the life of the church. Man-made denominational barriers are beginning to be broken down and God is working through ordinary individuals of all ages and walks to establish His Kingdom.

Our family is very blessed to serve at Raccoon Ford Christian Fellowship in Culpeper, Virginia under the very able leadership of Pastor Patrick J. Bopp and his lovely wife, Penny. Pastor Pat earned his masters degree at Kings College and Seminary, where Jack W. Hayford is founder and chancellor. Together Pastor Pat and Penny strive to be led by the Holy Spirit, seeking continuously to learn and move as He directs. Our church family is very loving and hungry for the things of God.

A vision exists to re-dig the wells of salvation on our land where, it is reported, 10,000 Civil War soldiers were saved during a revival.

As we learn to walk in Spiritual gifts, we are sharing them with churches in our area and in other nations as the Lord opens doors. Our youth, adults, and pastors have gone on missions to Haiti, Kenya, Mexico, Brazil, the Gulf Coast after hurricane Katrina and various other locations.

In our own church many have seen God heal physical problems, while others are being set free through "Prayer Ministry." We are also being greatly encouraged prophetically. I believe two keystones of our church are the multigenerational families and an exceptional group of young people. It especially touches my heart to see the hunger and excitement for God in our children, teenagers and young adults. They are growing in kingdom ministry along side our adults, often supplying scriptures, visions, prophetic words or words of knowledge and prayer for healing in our church services. All night prayer vigils are held about once a quarter with adult involvement. Our youth go out with an adult leader in the community to pray for people on the streets, in parks, in homes by knocking on doors, on the college campuses, and at hospitals. They also witness and pray in their schools and on the school buses. One day, as my feet were being prayed for, I felt a little hand on my shoulder and heard a small little voice praying in the spirit. I glanced over my shoulder and saw a six year old boy. My heart melted.

Seeing our youth praising God by jumping, twirling and rejoicing, and especially as they witness a healing, is wonderful. *Psalm 145:4 states, "One generation shall praise thy works to another and declare thy mighty acts."*

There are seven Hebrew words for praise including **halal** meaning: *"to be clear, to shine, to boast, show, to rave, celebrate, to be clamorously foolish."* Another is **yadah**: *"to throw out the hand, therefore to worship with extended hand"* and **barak**: *"to kneel down, to bless God as an act of adoration."* We are all learning to put these forms of worship into action.

Opportunities are given our young people to teach and lead worship for the congregation. Children from three years of age and up pray for and collect all our offerings.

As mentioned previously, my husband and I had the honor of being part of a team that ministered to 30-40 pastors in Mexico, witnessing the Lord's hand move in a mighty way. Absolutely nothing could be more fulfilling than being in His presence, serving Him, and seeing God work through us to establish His Kingdom here on earth.

You have turned for me my mourning into dancing; You have put off my sackcloth and clothed me with gladness, to the end that my glory may sing praise to You and not be silent. O Lord my God, I will give thanks to You forever.

(Psalm 30:11-12)

Salvation

Salvation that comes from trusting Christ which is what we preach is already within easy reach of each of us; in fact, it is as near as our own hearts and mouths. For if you tell others with your own mouth that Jesus Christ is your Lord, and believe in your own heart that God has raised Him from the dead, you will be saved. For it is by believing in his heart that a man becomes right with God; and with his mouth he tells others of his faith, confirming his salvation. For the Scriptures tell us that no one who believes in Christ will ever be disappointed. Jew and Gentile are the same in this respect: they all have the same Lord who generously gives His riches to all those who ask Him for them. Anyone who calls upon the name of the Lord will be saved. (Romans 10:8-13 TLB)

In addition to the numerous personal benefits of salvation, every person carries within them a unique purpose given by the Father. God has given believers 'giftings' to help establish His Kingdom here on earth. Repentance is to ask God's forgiveness for your sins and turn away from them, resulting in the removal of obstacles from your spiritual walk.

Lord, if you keep in mind our sins then who can ever get an answer to his prayers? But you forgive! What an awesome thing this is! (Psalm 130:3-4 TLB)

The measure of your repentance is the degree to which you will be able to move in spiritual principles.

David said, *"For I acknowledge my transgressions...Against You, You only, have I sinned... Behold, You desire truth in the inward parts, and in the hidden part You will make me to know wisdom"* (Psalm 51:3-4, 6).

While our sin has a ripple effect on those all around us, it is Father God who is the primary object of our sinfulness.

> *And there is no creature hidden from His sight, but all things are naked and open to the eyes of Him to whom we must give account.* (Hebrews 4:13)

God knows our every move and nothing is hidden from Him.

Perhaps you'd like to become a disciple of Jesus Christ and start learning how to walk in a powerful, glorious and abundant life. *"Salvation"* is translated from the Greek word **sozo** meaning: *"safe, to save, deliver, protect, heal, preserve, do well, to make whole."* By accepting Jesus you will receive God's grace (unmerited favor) for forgiveness of sin, eternal life, healing, deliverance, prosperity, and protection. These are free gifts provided by His son, Jesus Christ, at the cross. Would you like to ask God to forgive your sin? Would you like to invite Jesus into your heart, and receive Him as Savior?

Pray with me: *Father God*, I believe in my heart Jesus is Your Son and that You raised Him from the dead. I ask you to forgive me of my sins (take time to ask the Lord to bring your sins to mind, name them and with heartfelt repentance ask Him to forgive you of each one). Jesus, I ask You to come into my heart and be Savior of my soul and the Lord of my life. Fill me with the gift of Your Holy Spirit. In *Jesus'* name, amen. Now tell someone Jesus Christ is your Lord.

The next step is to make the Bible your closest friend. To become disciples we must study the Bible to learn how to walk in God's ways.

Jesus said...'If you abide in My word, you are My disciples indeed. And you shall know the truth and the truth shall make you free.' (John 8:31-32)

God communicates intimately with us through His Word. He can speak to each one of us in different, relevant and meaningful ways through the very same scripture.

For the Word that God speaks is alive and full of power [making it active, operative, energizing, and effective]: it is sharper than any two-edged sword, penetrating to the dividing line of the breath of life (soul) and [the immortal] spirit, and of joints and marrow [of the deepest parts of our nature], exposing and sifting and analyzing and judging the very thoughts and purposes of the heart.

(Hebrews 4:12 AMP)

111

His Word comes alive in our spirit, drawing us into the relationship and companionship God so desires. Intimacy with God should become our most important goal. It is prudent to ask God to give you a spiritual father or mother to help guide you on your walk. And look to other like-minded friends for fellowship and encouragement. God bless you in your Christian journey.

Billy Graham reads a chapter in Proverbs and five in Psalms to start his day. Find a passage of scripture to meditate on daily.

Your Word I have hidden in my heart, that I might not sin against you. (Psalm 119:11)

Years ago my friend Beverly, a teacher, made these suggestions to me. As you read the Bible, write out the verses that speak to you on 3x5 cards. Keep a few in your pocket to read now and then during the day. Soon you will find you know them by heart. Not only will they minister to you as you think about them but God will give you opportunities to minister encouragement to others through His Word.

My dentist very recently asked me how I knew I was saved and going to heaven. Humans have three parts: body, soul and spirit. When I accepted the Lord my spirit came alive. Being baptized with the gift of the Holy Spirit further energized me. I actually sensed a physical change inside my body. I was excited, joyful and had a feeling of lightness as my burdens lifted. I had peace in my heart. My whole focus in life changed. Now I had a purpose and a destiny. Co-workers noticed and said things like, *"Why are you so cheerful?"* One day I was by myself in a stock room pulling supplies for a surgery and feeling very happy. I was softly singing, *"The joy of the Lord is my strength..."* Oh, I felt so carefree. My supervisor asked, *"Are you okay?"* I guess she thought I'd lost it. Maybe it was my singing.

You can see life in the faces of Christians. They seem to have an extra twinkle in their eyes. My behavior and responses begin to reflect a more Christ-like attitude as I became familiar with God's Word. I began to understand the world in a new light. My salvation continues to be confirmed as prayers are answered and as I recognize God at work in the midst of my life. I know in my heart I am saved and have never looked back. The more I learn and experience God the more excited I get.

Through the Lord's mercies we are not consumed, because His compassions fail not. They are new every morning; great is Your faithfulness. "The Lord is my portion," says my soul, "Therefore I hope in Him!"

(Lamentations 3:22-24)

Holy Spirit

Isaiah 28:11-12 states: "For with stammering lips and another tongue He will speak to this people, To whom He said, "This is the rest with which You may cause the weary to rest," and, "This is the refreshing"; Yet they would not hear."

Isaiah 44:3-4 promises: "For I will pour water on him who is thirsty, and floods on the dry ground; I will pour My Spirit on your descendants, and My blessing on your offspring; They will spring up among the grass like willows by the watercourses."

Are you feeling a little dry and in need of an infusion of excitement in your walk with the Lord? Not only does the Holy Spirit refresh, He brings boldness and power to your ministry. The baptism in the Holy Spirit causes Satan to tremble. It is such a powerful gift! Don't let the devil thimblerig (to cheat by trickery) you from receiving this vital spiritual prayer weapon. Being a seamstress, I know the most sensitive part of my hand is my fingertips. When I think of being rigged with a thimble, I know that no feelings can go into or come from my finger. This is a good thing for a seamstress. Be aware the devil will try to desensitize you in anyway he can to the powerful working of the Holy Spirit. Asking for the infilling of the Spirit will increase your sensitivity to the things of God. It will give you a deeper understanding and possible participation in the other gifts of the Spirit for your own spiritual development, fulfillment, and contribution to the edifying and ministry of the body of Christ.

The baptism in the Holy Spirit is a spiritual gift separate from the indwelling of the Holy Spirit we receive when we accept Jesus. This gift gives you power, boldness, a personal spiritual language (also called tongues) as well as many other blessings.

Spiritual language is a form of speaking or singing to God in prayer, praise, adoration, or giving thanks. The gift of tongues is a unique heavenly language you have not learned. Tongues spoken in a church setting is a form of this gifting meant to be interpreted so all can hear and be edified. It is a message from God. Praying privately in tongues is the Holy Spirit praying perfectly through you to the Father. The gift of interpretation of tongues can be used both privately and publicly but most often is used publicly.

Good reasons for praying in tongues daily:

1. Follow the Biblical example.

> *...Peter and John...when they had come down, prayed for them that they might receive the Holy Spirit. For as yet He had fallen upon none of them. They had only been baptized in the name of the Lord Jesus. Then they laid hands on them and they received the Holy Spirit.* (Acts 8:14-17)

'Did you receive the Holy Spirit when you believed?' So they said to him, 'We have not so much as heard whether there is a Holy Spirit. 'Into what were you were baptized?' So they said, 'Into John's baptism.' Then Paul said, 'John indeed baptized with a baptism of repentance...that they should believe on...Christ Jesus.' When they heard this, they were baptized in the name of the Lord Jesus. And when Paul had laid hands on them, the Holy Spirit came upon them, and they spoke with tongues and prophesied.

(Acts 19:2-6)

Jesus said: *"these signs will follow those who believe: In My name they will cast out demons; they will speak with new tongues...they will lay hands on the sick and they will recover" (Mark 16:17-18).*

*And they were **all** filled with the Holy Spirit and began to speak with other tongues, as the Spirit gave them utterance.* *(Acts 2:4)*

2. Build your faith and become spiritually strong.

But you, beloved, building yourselves up on your most holy faith, praying in the Holy Spirit. *(Jude 20)*

He who speaks in a tongue edifies himself.

(I Corinthians 14:4)

117

Jesus said: *"You shall receive power when the Holy Spirit has come upon you..."* *(Acts 1:8).*

3. Pray the will of God in intercessory prayer.

...the Spirit also helps in our weaknesses for we do not know what we should pray for as we ought, but the Spirit Himself makes intercession for us with groanings which cannot be uttered. Now He who searches the hearts knows what the mind of the Spirit is, because He makes intercession for the saints according to the will of God.

(Romans 8:26-27)

4. The Holy Spirit is our Teacher and Comforter.

But the Helper (and Comforter), *the Holy Spirit, whom the Father will send in My Name, He will teach you all things, and bring to your remembrance all things that I said to you.* *(John 14:26)*

Ask Jesus to fill you with His Holy Spirit. It is a free gift available today to every believer. *Luke 11:13 "If you then, being evil, know how to give good gifts to your children, how much more will your heavenly Father give the Holy Spirit to those who ask Him!"* Ask Him to forgive your sins, renounce all things of the occult, and false teaching concerning the Holy Spirit. Then ask the Holy Spirit to give you a new language. God usually does not take over your tongue, you must speak out syllables and words that you do not recognize. The Lord will take your act of faith and give you His new language. Or, you may start by praising Him until you are able to loose your tongue with your new spiritual language. Sometimes it comes as a full language but most likely it will first come in small syllables. This new language may seem odd but don't let the enemy try to convince you it is not real. As you pursue it you will soon find it feels natural and flows easily. I challenge you to reap the benefits by starting your morning praying in the Holy Spirit and then use the gift as often as you can throughout the day.

When couples pray together in the Spirit, there is extra power. *Ecclesiastes 4:12 "Though one may be overpowered by another, two can withstand him, and a threefold cord is not quickly broken."* Imagine the two of you and the Holy Spirit in agreement. Awesome! Several years back Gary and I were asked at a marriage retreat to face each other, hold hands, then pray for 45 minutes in the Spirit. It seemed like an eternity but it broke through a barrier that the enemy tries to use to keep couples from praying together in tongues. For a long period of time after that Gary set the alarm at 4:45 a.m. so we could pray together before he left for work. We would pray for about 30 minutes, half the time in English, the other half in the Spirit. You will unfurl a great adventure. We use this routine on and off through the years. *Deuteronomy 32:30* speaks to the power of unity: *"one (can) chase a thousand, and two put ten thousand to flight."*

My husband and I also often pray when driving. We start by praising the Lord together inviting the Holy Spirit in our midst, *"so that times of refreshing may come from the presence of the Lord" (Acts 3:19).* Then, generally one of us prays in English while the other prays in the Spirit. Sometimes we both pray together in the Spirit and let the Holy Spirit apply the prayer where needed. *"He who speaks in a tongue does not speak to man but to God, for no one understands him; however in the spirit he speaks mysteries." (I Corinthians 14:2)*

Spiritual warfare takes place in prayer and praying in the Holy Spirit is one of our weapons.

For the weapons of our warfare are not carnal but mighty in God for pulling down strongholds, casting down arguments and every high thing that exalts itself against the knowledge of God, bringing every thought into captivity to the obedience of Christ. (2 Corinthians 10:4-5)

For we do not wrestle against flesh and blood, but against principalities, against powers, against the rulers of the darkness of this age, against spiritual hosts of wickedness in the heavenly places; therefore take up the whole armor of God, that you may be able to withstand in the evil day, and having done all, to stand...above all, taking the shield of faith with which you will be able to quench all the fiery darts of the wicked one...and take the helmet of salvation, and the sword of the Spirit, which is the word of God;

*praying always with all prayer and supplication **in the Spirit.*** *(Ephesians 6:12-18)*

Praying in tongues builds up our armor, strengthens our faith and launches effective offensive or defensive weapons against Satan. Personally I would rather be prayed up and on the offensive side. Amen! *1 Peter 5:8 "Be sober, be vigilant; because your adversary the devil walks about like a roaring lion, seeking whom he may devour."*

When praying in tongues it is nice to pray through your request until you sense a peace. My prayer language often changes in tone either to praise or warfare. To me this indicates either an answer, completion, or more prayer is needed. At times a scripture, word, phrase or name will come to mind helping to direct or answer prayer. The Holy Spirit is with us at all times and available for counsel. When you speak with the Holy Spirit He will respond to you.

May God bless you: *"as you earnestly desire the best gifts"* *(1Corinthians12:31).*

EXPERIENCE
THE
power of prayer

Nutrition Notes

*E*ach day every human is exposed to bacteria, viruses and carcinogens. I have GREAT NEWS! God created us with an awesome magnificent immune system to throw off these invaders. When properly nourished our immune system can prevent and is most often able to reverse cancer, diabetes, heart and many other diseases. Modern (?) medicine often wants to kill the immune system. We don't get sick by accident and most likely we won't get well without intentionally pursuing God's plan for our food. This, of course, is in addition to drawing close to Him through His Word and prayer, forgiveness, fellowship, laughter, exercise, sunshine, sleep, water, and a thankful heart. And, I praise God for doctors, if needed. All work together and are dependent on one another for good health.

Let's hear what a few of our forefathers had to say: *"Let thy food be thy medicine and thy medicine be thy food,"* Hippocrates, the father of medicine, 4th century B.C.

"The doctor of the future will give no medicine, but will interest his patients in the care of the human frame, in diet and in the cause and prevention of diseases," Thomas Edison.

"Each patient carries his own doctor inside him," Albert Schweitzer, Nobel Prize winner.

"...Nobody today can say that one does not know what cancer and its prime cause is. On the contrary, there is no disease whose prime cause is better known, so that today ignorance is no longer an excuse that one cannot do more about prevention," Dr. Otto Warburg, Nobel Prize winner.

The cells in our bodies are constantly being replaced by new ones. It is crucial to eat the right food so new cells have the correct nourishment to keep our organs and immune system in peak condition and able to resist disease. We may think we are eating right. But whom have we learned from? Most of us have been influenced by family habits, television, our culture, public information (constantly changing and often incorrect), and the almost complete lack of the teaching of nutrition in our medical schools. God gives us guidelines in the first chapter of the bible. *God said, See, I have given you every plant yielding seed that is on the face of all the land and every tree with seed in its fruit; you shall have them for food. (Genesis 1:29 AMP)*

Why did those early saints live to be 900+ years? After the flood of Noah's day, meat was introduced, sin increased and the age span of man declined quickly down through the generations to David who lived to be seventy years old. How about the four young Jewish men that were taken to serve in King Nebuchadnezzar's palace? These young men were very intelligent, good looking, and quick learners. They were instructed to eat the rich food and wine of the king as part of their training. According to Jewish dietary laws they asked to eat only vegetables. Contrary to popular opinion vegetables have protein and some more than meat.

Please test your servants for ten days, and let them give us vegetables to eat and water to drink. (Daniel 1:12)

At the end of ten days their features appeared better and fatter in flesh than all the young men who ate the portion of the king's delicacies. (Daniel 1:15-20)

The four young men obeyed the laws of God and He gave them: *"knowledge and skill in all literature and wisdom... And in all matters of wisdom and understanding about which the king examined them, he found them ten times better than all the magicians and astrologers who were in all his realm"* (Daniel 1:15-20).

Eating the wrong foods can be likened to putting the wrong oil or poor gas in your car. Your car will break down sooner than expected. Another example of the laws of nature is found in my rose garden experiences.

I had 40 patented rosebushes in one of my gardens in California. I picked a location with plenty of sunshine, dug very deep holes and put in good soil and nutrients to make a nice bed before planting. I pampered them with plenty of water, rose food at regular intervals, and a proper pruning every year. They flourished and provided me with plenty of beautiful blooms.

My present rose garden had a different start. I purchased the healthiest plants as I had before, but over time they developed deformed leaves, had few blossoms and some even died. The difference was the rocky, clay-like, nutrient deficient soil, which also made it difficult to dig a big hole. I had trouble finding a place with enough sunshine (essential for roses and humans). I soon learned there are no shortcuts. We cut down a tree, dug very deep holes, put in good soil and nutrients, regularly fed them the proper rose food and once again we have happy beautiful roses.

The biggest obstacle my husband and I had to overcome with our eating habits was our mind-set. We firmly believed we were eating a healthy diet, but soon found we needed improvement. When told about diet as a way to reverse disease we jumped right in the next day. After four years I can truly say we thoroughly enjoy the great variety of our meals and do not miss the foods we thought we "had" to have. We are very pleased with the results. We opted for a prayer and nutritional approach following a needle biopsy diagnosis of prostate cancer in Gary. He has regular checkups by specialists and the two growths are no longer palpable. Gary is healthy with no medical intervention. It is a continuous process of reading, learning, and adjusting. My awe of God has increased through my learning how He has provided us with readily accessible foods for sustaining good health.

He causes the grass to grow for the cattle and vegetation for the service of man, that he may bring forth food from the earth. *(Psalm 104:14)*

We have heard hundreds of amazing testimonies of people (including medical doctors), reversing devastating diseases through God's natural remedies alone. This includes forgiveness, diet, water, sunshine (at least 15-30 min/day to get vitamin D), and so forth as mentioned previously.

Much of the church, with the exception of the Seventh Day Adventist (who live an average of 7-10 years longer according to a Nov. 2005 report in National Geographic), seemingly do not make the connection between nutrition and disease. I find it curious that we ask God to heal us, as we should, but often are not interested in learning or assuming our responsibility in the stewardship of our bodies. Our diets can and often do leave us vulnerable to disease. It is such good news to know God gave us a wonderful array of colorful delicious food to prevent and cure disease in a natural way. To be able to offer hope to someone, when he or she may have been told there is none, is downright exciting! Bon Appetite! Please be advised I am not negating the role of medicine and its necessity, at times, to facilitate healing. However, the underlying cause of disease must be treated and prevention taught.

References that helped us get started on good nutrition:

1. Hallelujah Acres was started by Dr. George Malkmus, who was healed of colon cancer through nutrition alone. It has a large following, extensive testimonials, good videos/DVDs, books (we first read *God's Way to Ultimate Health*), and a great website, www.Hacres.com.

2. Lorraine Day, MD overcame invasive breast cancer the natural way, has a number of very good and well-researched videos/DVDs including *You Can't Improve on God* and *Cancer Doesn't Scare Me Anymore*. www.DrDay.com

3. ***The China Study*** by T. Colin Campbell, PhD, and Thomas Campbell II; 2005, BenBella Books, is excellent, the culmination of 70 grant-years of peer reviewed research and the most comprehensive study of nutrition ever conducted on diet and it's correlation to disease. Dr. T. Colin Campbell is Professor Emeritus of Nutritional Biochemistry at Cornell University. ***A must read!***

4. *Green for Life*, a book, or *Greens Can Save Your Life*, a DVD, by Victoria Boutenko, is very worthwhile for the "green smoothie" information. www.RawFamily.com

5. *Healing Cancer From the Inside Out* and *Eating 2nd Edition-plus* by Michael Anderson are very informative DVDs.

6. For encouraging information and resource people to talk with, the websites of Dr. John McDougall and Dr. Max Gerson, are helpful.

Memory Verses

*H*ere are some great verses handpicked with the help of family and friends as acknowledged. God's Word is our fuel and a weapon in our hands. All scripture is from the New King James Version unless noted.

Old Testament

Genesis 50:20 *"…God turned into good what you meant for evil, for He brought me to this high position I have today so that I could save the lives of many."* TLB

Robert and Chantal Gilliam, Beirut, Lebanon

Exodus 23:25 *"… you shall serve the Lord your God, and He will bless your bread and your water. 'And I will take sickness away from the midst of you.'"*

Leviticus 11:44 *"I am the Lord your God. you shall therefore consecrate yourselves, and you shall be holy; for I am holy."*

Kent and Mary Alice Martin, Birmingham, England

Numbers 23:19 *"God is not a man, that He should lie. He doesn't change His mind…Has He ever promised, without doing what He said?"* TLB

Deuteronomy 29:29 *"The secret things belong to the Lord our God, but those things which are revealed belong to us and to our children forever, that we may do all the words of this law."* Marion Hauser, NC

Joshua 1:9 *"Have I not commanded you? Be strong and of good courage; do not be afraid, nor be dismayed, for the Lord your God is with you wherever you go."*

Mac Bridger, Treverton, Devon England

Judges 6:12 *"And the Angel of the Lord appeared to him* [Gideon], *and said to him, 'The Lord is with you, you mighty man of valor!'"*

Ruth 1:16 *"Ruth said: 'Entreat me not to leave you, or to turn back from following after you; for wherever you go I will go; and where ever you lodge, I will lodge; your people shall be my people, and your God, my God.'"* Victoria Harrell, VA

1 Samuel 16:7 *"...For the Lord does not see as man sees; for man looks at the outward appearance, but the Lord looks at the heart."* Gloria Stendal, Bogota, Colombia

2 Samuel 6:14 *"David danced before the Lord with all his might..."*

1 Kings 17:21-22 *"And he* (Elijah) *stretched himself out on the child three times, and cried out to the Lord and said, 'O Lord my God, I pray, let this child's soul come back to him.' Then the Lord heard the voice of Elijah; and the soul of the child came back to him, and he revived."*

2 Kings 6:17 *"And Elisha prayed, and said, 'Lord, I pray, open his eyes that he may see.' Then the Lord opened the eyes of the young man, and he saw. And behold, the mountain was full of horses and chariots of fire all around Elisha."*

1 Chronicles 28:9 *"As for you, my son Solomon, know the God of your father, and serve Him with a loyal heart and with a willing mind; for the Lord searches all hearts and understands all the intent of the thoughts. If you seek Him, He will be found by you; but if you forsake Him, He will cast you off forever."*

2 Chronicles 16:9 *"For the eyes of the Lord run to and fro throughout the whole earth, to show Himself strong on behalf of those whose heart is loyal to Him."* Nellie Santinga, VA

Ezra 7:10 *"…Ezra had prepared his heart to seek the Law of the Lord, and to do it, and to teach statutes and ordinances in Israel."*

Nehemiah 8:10 *"…Do not sorrow, for the joy of the Lord is your strength."* Barbara Owens, VA

Esther 4:14 *"For if you remain completely silent at this time, relief and deliverance will arise for the Jews from another place, but you and your father's house will perish. Yet who knows whether you have come to the kingdom for such a time as this?"* Pastor Patrick Bopp, VA

Job 42:10 *"...the Lord restored Job's losses when he prayed for his friends, indeed the Lord gave Job twice as much as he had before."*

Psalm 51:10-12 *"Create in me a clean heart, O God, and renew a steadfast spirit within me. Do not cast me away from Your presence, and do not take Your Holy Spirit from me. Restore to me the joy of Your salvation, and uphold me with Your generous Spirit."* Will Hart, missionary Mozambique, Africa

Proverbs 3:5, 6 *"Trust in the Lord with all your heart, and lean not on your own understanding; in all your ways acknowledge Him, and He shall direct your paths."* Nataliya Ryabko, Tynda, Amur Region, Russia

Ecclesiastes 12: 13-14 *"Fear God and keep His commandments, for this is the whole duty of man. For God will bring every work into judgment, including every secret thing, whether it is good or whether it is evil."* Judith Hoppe, CA

Song of Solomon 2:4 *"He brought me to the banqueting house, and His banner over me was love."* Aimee Elizabeth Stevens, VA

Isaiah 41:9-10 " '*You whom I have taken from the ends of the earth, and called from its farthest regions,' and said to you, 'You are My servant, I have chosen you and have not cast you away: fear not, for I am with you; be not dismayed, for I am your God. I will strengthen you, yes, I will help you, I will uphold you with My righteous right hand.'*"

Pastor Tom Hauser, NC

Isaiah 45:3 "*I will give you the treasures of darkness and hidden riches of secret places, that you may know that I, the Lord, who call you by your name, Am the God of Israel.*"

Pastor Priscilla Reid Belfast, Ireland

Jeremiah 33:3 "*Call to Me, and I will answer you, and show you great and mighty things, which you do not know.*"

Doris Harris, New Zealand

Lamentations 3:22, 23 "*Through the Lord's mercies we are not consumed, because His compassions fail not. They are new every morning, great is your faithfulness.*" Nellie Santinga, VA

Ezekiel 36:26-27 "*I will give you a new heart and put a new spirit within you; I will take the heart of stone out of your flesh and give you a heart of flesh. I will put My Spirit within you and cause you to walk in My statutes, and you will keep My judgments and do them.*"

Anna Gabrielle (Stevens) Denniston, VA

Daniel 3:17, 25 *"...our God whom we serve is able to deliver us from the burning fiery furnace,...Look!...I see four men loose, walking in the midst of the fire; and they are not hurt, and the form of the fourth is like the Son of God."*

Beverly Bel Cher, CA

Hosea 6:3 *"Let us know, let us pursue the knowledge of the Lord. His going forth is established as the morning; He will come to us like the rain..."*

Joel 2:13 *"So rend your heart, and not your garments; Return to the Lord your God, for He is gracious and merciful, slow to anger, and of great kindness; and He relents from doing harm."*

Connie Markva, VA

Amos 3:3 *"Can two walk together, unless they are agreed?"*

Connie Markva, VA

Obadiah 3-4 *"The pride of your heart has deceived you...You who say in your heart, who will bring me down to the ground? Though you exalt yourself as high as the eagle, and though you set your nest among the stars, from there I will bring you down, says the Lord."*

Jonah 2:2 *"I cried out to the Lord because of my affliction, and He answered me."*

Joanie Oesterreicher, VA

Micah 6:8 *"He has shown you, O man, what is good, and what does the Lord require of you but to do justly, to love mercy, and to walk humbly with your God?"*

Joanie Oesterreicher, VA

Nahum 1:7 *"The Lord is good, a stronghold in the day of trouble; and He knows those who trust in Him."*

Habakkuk 3:18, 19 *"...I will rejoice in the Lord, I will be happy in the God of my salvation. The Lord God is my Strength, and He will give me the speed of a deer and bring me safely over the mountains."* TLB

Gary Stevens, VA

Zephaniah 3:17 *"The Lord your God in your midst, the Mighty One, will save; He will rejoice over you with gladness, He will quiet you in His love, He will rejoice over you with singing."*

Pat Searle, VA

Haggai 2:5 *"According to the word that I covenanted with you when you came out of Egypt, so My Spirit remains among you; do not fear!"*

Zechariah 4:6, 7 *"...This is the word of the Lord to Zerubbabel: 'Not by might nor by power, but by My Spirit,' says the Lord of hosts. 'Who are you, O great mountain? Before Zerubbabel you shall become a plain! And he shall bring forth the capstone with shouts of "Grace, grace to it!"'"*

Stephanie Stevens, NC

Malachi 4:2 *"But to you who fear My name, the Sun of Righteousness shall arise with healing in His wings."*

Gary Stevens, VA

New Testament

Matthew 19:26 *"With men this is impossible but with God all things are possible."*

Bobbie Assur, VA

Mark 11:25, 26 *"And whenever you stand praying, if you have anything against anyone, forgive him, that your Father in heaven may also forgive you your trespasses. But if you do not forgive, neither will your Father in heaven forgive your trespasses."*

Lance Kevin Stevens, MN

Luke 6:45 *"A good man out of the good treasure of his heart brings forth good; and an evil man out the evil treasure of his heart brings forth evil. For out of the abundance of the heart the mouth speaks."*

Shawn Christian Stevens, NC

John 17:4 *"I have glorified You on the earth. I have finished the work which You have given Me to do."*

Marilyn Hughes, Saltillo, Mexico

Acts 2:28 *"You have made known to me the ways of life; You will enrapture me (diffusing my soul with joy) with and in Your presence."* AMP

Suzanne Fletcher, VA

Romans 8:38-39 *"For I am persuaded that neither death nor life, nor angels nor principalities nor powers, nor things present nor things to come, nor height nor depth, nor any other created thing, shall be able to separate us from the love of God which is in Christ Jesus our Lord."*

Donna Nafizer, Wellesley, Ontario, Canada

1 Corinthians 13:1 *"Though I speak with the tongues of men and of angels, but have not love, I have become as sounding brass or a clanging cymbal."* Danya Hancock, CO

2 Corinthians 1:3-4 *"Blessed be the God and Father of our Lord Jesus Christ, the Father of mercies and God of all comfort, who comforts us in all our tribulation, that we may be able to comfort those who are in any trouble, with the comfort with which we ourselves are comforted by God."*

Sheila Blount, VA

Galatians 5:22, 23 *"...the fruit of the Spirit is love, joy, peace, longsuffering, kindness, goodness, faithfulness, gentleness, self-control. Against such there is no law."* Jan Beveridge, VA

Ephesians 3:20 *"Now to Him who is able to do exceedingly abundantly above all that we ask or think, according to the power that works in us."* Mel and Maria Howard, CO

Philippians 2:12, 14-15 *"...work out your own salvation with fear and trembling ...Do all things without murmuring and disputing, that you may become blameless and harmless, children of God without fault in the midst of a crooked and perverse generation, among whom you shine as lights in the world."* Addie Bonsignore, NC

Colossians 1:13 *"He has delivered us from the power of darkness and translated us into the kingdom of the Son of His love, in whom we have redemption through His blood, the forgiveness of sins."* Pastor Patrick Bopp, VA

1 Thessalonians 5:16,17,18 *"Rejoice always, pray without ceasing, in everything give thanks; for this is the will of God in Christ Jesus for you."* Gary Stevens, VA

2 Thessalonians 3:13 *"...brethren, do not grow weary in doing good."*

1 Timothy 4:12 *"Let no one despise your youth, but be an example to the believers in word, in conduct, in love, in spirit, in faith, in purity."* Kevin Denniston, VA

2 Timothy 3:16-17 *"All scripture is given by inspiration of God, and is profitable for doctrine, for reproof, for correction, for instruction in righteousness, that the man of God may be complete, thoroughly equipped for every good work."*

Titus 3:2 *"...speak evil of no one...be peaceable, gentle, showing all humility to all men."* Lisa Stevens, MN

Philemon 6 *"...pray that as you share your faith with others it will grip their lives too, as they see the wealth of good things in you that come from Christ Jesus."* TLB

Hebrews 13:8 *"Jesus Christ is the same yesterday, today and forever!"* Beverly Bel Cher, CA

James 5:13-15 *"Is anyone among you suffering? Let him pray. Is anyone cheerful? Let him sing psalms. Is anyone among you sick? Let him call for the elders of the church and let them pray over him, anointing him with oil in the name of the Lord. And the prayer of faith will save the sick, and the Lord will raise him up..."* Vivian Patrick, CA

1 Peter 4:10 *"As each one has received a gift, minister it to one another, as good stewards of the manifold grace of God."* The Szymanski Family, Shanghai, China

2 Peter 1:5, 6, 7 *"...giving all diligence, add to your faith virtue, to virtue knowledge, to knowledge self-control, to self-control perseverance, to perseverance godliness, to godliness brotherly kindness, and to brotherly kindness love."* Adam Assur, VA

1 John 4:4 *"You are of God, little children, and have overcome them, because He who is in you is greater than he who is in the world."*   Joanna Guth, Acheiin, Germany

2 John 5, 6 *"...love one another. This is love, that we walk according to His commandments. This is the commandment, that as you have heard from the beginning, you should walk in it."*

3 John 4 *"I have no greater joy than to hear that my children walk in truth."*

Jude 24-25 *"Now to Him who is able to keep you from stumbling, and to present you faultless before the presence of His glory with exceeding joy, to God our savior, who alone is wise, be glory and majesty, dominion and power, both now and forever. Amen."*   Pastor Carol Arnott, Toronto, Ontario, Canada

Revelation 4:11 *"You are worthy, O Lord, to receive glory and honor and power; for You created all things, and by Your will they exist and were created."*

Prayers

Generational Blessing from Fathers to Children:

I love you my daughter / my son. You are uniquely gifted and I believe there is nothing in your heart that you cannot accomplish. There are not enough words to tell you how special you are to me. I am honored to be your father. I will support you in *every* endeavor you undertake. I commission you into your God given purposes and destiny asking for His blessing on all aspects of your life. I release angels to keep you in all your ways. I cancel any negative curse spoken against you or our family line. You are loved beyond measure and you will always have a secure place in my heart. All the love I have in my heart I pour into yours.
I love you,

Dad

_____

Prayers

Prayer for your children

Well documented are the results of praying mothers, fathers, and grandparents. I recommend covering your children/grandchildren daily. Here is a scriptural guide I use for my children:

Dear *Father God,*

I pray in the name of Jesus Christ ___ would move under the banner of Your will, be filled with all the love and fullness of You, God, and be strengthened with might through Your Spirit in (his/her) inner man.

(Ephesians 3:16-21)

I pray that through Your Word the mind of Jesus Christ will be imprinted upon the mind, will and heart of ___.

___ is becoming a vessel of honor, sanctified, useful to the Master and prepared for every good work. *(2 Timothy 2:21)*

May the Lord God give ___ the tongue of the learned that (he/she) should know how to speak a word in season to him who is weary. God awakens ___ morning by morning. He awakens ___ ear to hear as the learned. Lord God open ___ ear; ___ is not rebellious, and does not turn away from You.

(Isaiah 50:4-5)

Lord I make a wall and stand in the gap on behalf of ___, that (he/she) will not be destroyed or settle for less than Your best plan for (his/her) life. *(Ezekiel 22:30)*

142

I thank you for loving ___ and know You have good plans of peace to give ___ a future and a hope.   *(Jeremiah 29:11)*

I ask you to send forth Your ministering spirits for ___ protection and to cover ___ with the blood of Jesus from the crown of (his/her) head to the bottom of (his/her) feet.

Release the power of the blood of Jesus upon ___ to reveal Your Truth. May Your Truth set ___ free to choose You, Jesus, not only as Savior of (his/her) soul but as Lord of (his/her) life.   *(John 8:32)*

In the name of *Jesus*, amen!